How NOT to Murder your ADHD Kid

How NOT to Murder your ADHD Kid

Instead learn how to be
your child's own ADHD Coach

Sarah Templeton

www.HeadstuffADHDLiberty.co.uk
www.HeadstuffADHDTherapy.co.uk

Illustrations by Sarah Scott Logos & Design

Cover design by Proactive Edge

Published 2021
Second edition, updated and improved 2022
Published by Gemini Publishing Ltd.

ISBN: 978-1-7399588-0-0

ACKNOWLEDGEMENTS

This book came into existence because of two strong women who, like me, never gave up.

The first was Moira; my fantastic tutor at counselling college who fought more battles for me than any tutor ever should have to. She stuck her neck out for me on more than one occasion to get me through my counselling training which, being undiagnosed ADHD at the time, was torturously tedious and reduced me to tears on many occasions - my short-term memory just not being up to the task of remembering the great paragraphs of corrections I was being asked to do.

But Moira never gave up on me. Even when an unscrupulous supposed 'professional' - working within the prison service - decided to outrightly lie on my college course paperwork, it was Moira who counteracted the whole lot with the awarding body.

She also hollered in the face of this same uncaring person who COULD NOT SEE that all I was trying to do was help young offenders, as I sat and sobbed as she stripped me of my prison belt and keys and took me away from my beloved boys.[1] But Moira could see it.

She also gave me the best piece of advice that has stood me in great stead with hundreds of offenders since.

"Always be on their side Sarah," she said, "Always let them know that you are on their side."

Moira, I will never be able to thank you enough.

Very shortly after I left Moira's college I began with a new counsellor, Lynda. It was Lynda who, on session 3, said to me these now famous words.

---

[1] Nobody kept me away from my prison boys. I wrote to every single one of them, visited them in all the prisons they were shipped out to all over the UK, and I'm still in touch with pretty much all of them to this day.

"Has anybody ever suggested you are ADHD?"

I was fifty-one. I looked at her with my eyebrows raised and said "No! why?"

"Because I think you are," she retorted. "Go home and Google it and tell me what you think next week."

I did and after about two-hundred lightbulb moments and my entire life dropping into place that night, I tootled off to the NHS - twice - to be told both times "there is no money in the NHS for adult ADHD".

I reported this back to Lynda my counsellor who was not impressed and told me I should 'go Private'.

After returning from seeing a private ADHD psychiatrist in London who had told me *'I couldn't possibly be ADHD because I wasn't diagnosed as a child'* Lynda accepted this for about five minutes in our next session before exploding.

"I'm sorry but this is bollocks - you are ADHD". She just wasn't going to accept that I wasn't ADHD and without her firm boot up my bottom I would never have pursued that diagnosis that has gone on to change my life.

Not only moderate to severe ADHD but three of its comorbidities - severe dyspraxia, dyscalculia, and sensory processing disorder. All of these conditions had affected me all my life but without Lynda being so sure and resolute about getting me diagnosed, I would never have reached the understanding of myself that I now have, in my late fifties.

Lynda then went on to supervise me for five years as I learnt my ADHD trade working with hundreds of ADHD kids, adolescents, and adults. I learnt more about ADHD from this lady than anyone else. I literally owe her my life. I would never have made sense of my life without her.

CONTENTS

WHAT SOME ADHD PROFESSIONALS HAVE SAID ABOUT SARAH TEMPLETON

"I just wanted you to know that the young man we sent you was hugely influenced by his time with you. You changed his whole outlook and attitude to ADHD. He is now very accepting of it and open to the help we are offering him. We could not have done this without your input."
Andrea Bilbow, The National Attention Deficit Disorder Information and Support Service, ADDISS

"Sarah understands ADHD from the inside out and is passionate about turning kids lives around."
Dr Helen Read, Psychiatrist, The ADHD Consultancy

"I have recommended Sarah a number of times to clients needing ADHD Therapy – for her 'no nonsense', 'say it as it is' approach."
Soli Lazarus. B.Ed (Hons) Psychology, Yellow Sun

"You won't find another book like this. Written by an experienced counsellor with ADHD who really understands ADHD kids and how to get the best out of them."
Dr Sawhney, ADHD Specialist Paediatrician

"Sarah is an expert in all things ADHD. She works so successfully with ADHD Clients because she understands the condition from the inside out."
Dr Jose Belda, ADHD Psychiatrist

AND NOW WHAT PARENTS AND CLIENTS THEMSELVES HAVE TO SAY

"Sarah literally saved our sons life. School, doctors and CAMHS did not. Without her counselling we would not be where we are today."
Mum ADHD son, 18

"I have referred clients to Sarah and value her professional opinion on clients who I suspect have ADHD. She's never been wrong. Her vast experience in this area has gone a long way to helping people make sense of their lives."
BACP Counsellor, Dorset

"At first I didn't want to see Sarah. I've seen so many rubbish counsellors over the years. But Sarah is totally different. She really understands my ADHD.

My dream has always been to be a footballer, but I'd just been arrested before I saw Sarah and was under investigation. I thought I'd totally ruined my life. Sarah convinced me to still follow my dreams and never give up. When I was offered a football trial my anxiety made me nearly turn it down, but I asked Sarah if she would come and she did. On a very dark rainy Monday night.

I've now been offered a two-year apprenticeship with a professional football club which coincided with the week the police dropped their charges. I now feel totally confident and happy within myself and I never did before."
ADHD Boy, 16

"After 10 years being treated for an eating disorder by a very expensive psychologist, it took ONE SESSION for Sarah to realise that my eating issues were due to ADHD and compulsive eating. I'm now finally on the right path to understanding my issues."
ADHD Lady, 62

"I highly recommend Sarah Templeton and the team at Headstuff Therapy. Sarah is really passionate about working with ADHD children experiencing difficulties and they all love her."
ADHD Psychiatrist.

"My 16-year-old son refused to see Sarah at first saying he'd only tell her to "f**k off" if he didn't like her. She passed the message back through me that he needn't worry, she would tell him exactly the same if she didn't like him!

This intrigued and impressed him enough to see her and several months of therapy with her later - he now thinks of Sarah as one of his best mates!"

Mum, ADHD/Dyspraxia Boy, 16

"Sarah first recognised ADHD in me when I wasn't even there to see her about it! I'm now diagnosed in my mid 40s and as a teacher I am now ADHD-aware enough to spot ADHD in my classroom. Sarah 'gets it'. She has been a tremendous help to me personally and professionally and this book will be a great resource for parents of ADHD children who need a helping hand."

Suzanne, 48, Berkshire

"Sarah is quite simply The Queen of ADHD!! Some medical professionals are qualified up to their armpits and think they know all about ADHD but they really don't. Sarah is qualified, experienced and a walking genius on us ADHDers because she's got it herself."

Teacher, 32, Berkshire

"Sarah was not only there for our diagnosed son, she also recognised ADHD in my other son and she has been there for the whole family during our most difficult times."

Mum, ADHD/ASD sons, 21 & 17

"It's not until you meet someone who truly understands ADHD that you truly understand yourself. Without Sarah I would still be blaming myself for so many things that I now know can be attributed to my late ADHD diagnosis."

Steve Lodge, Physiotherapist, High Wycombe

"In our most difficult times, all doors seem to be closed. Sarah's door opened a new world for our son. No words can describe what this meant for us."

Mother, son 18

"Nothing you can do or say will shock Sarah. She is totally non-judgmental about ADHD and nothing you could say will faze her. She makes you realise "actually I'm not a complete nutter and my children aren't either".

It's like a light bulb moment when you meet and talk to Sarah – suddenly everything you ever did makes sense and you are no longer alone with your own thoughts. She also puts a network of support around you with the Adult ADHD support group she set up."

Louise, 42, High Wycombe

"Sarah's empathy and understanding of my ADHD gained my trust in her which was key to helping me change."

ADHD Girl, 20

"Sarah worked out in one session that my son's eating problems were connected to ADHD when other professionals hadn't. And at the same time she recognised ADHD in me - his Dad. She put us both on the path to assessment, diagnosis and medication and in one fell swoop changed our lives for the better."

ADHD Dad 39 & Son 10

"Sarah could empathise with my ADHD teenage son like no other therapist."

Mum. ADHD son, 19

"There is a real lack of therapists who understand ADHD like Sarah does. She is very passionate and amazing at her job and I am not surprised she is so incredibly busy."

Mum, ADHD/ASD son, 21

"Sarah's understanding of my ADHD and being totally non-judgmental about my criminal past (which had got me into BIG trouble twice) has made me wish that the rest of our system could be as understanding as her."

ADHD Boy, 19

"My son struggled all through his teens. He never settled at school. CAMHSwrote him off with 'behavioural problems'. Until the amazing Sarah Templeton recognised his ADHD and ASD."

Mum ADHD/ASD Boy, 23

"I can confidently add 'Meeting Sarah Templeton' to my life-changing events! After meeting Sarah I had a whole new perspective on what ADHD means for me and my whole family."

ADHD Mum, ADHD sons 13 & 15

"I can't thank you enough - my son has just rung me to say, 'how can someone understand how I tick so quickly? Nobody has ever understood me apart from Sarah.' Thank you. Thank you."

Mum, Undiagnosed ADHD Son, 37

"I think that letter you read to my son yesterday from an actual prisoner about how horrific prison is, had a real impact on him. Fingers crossed it stays with him. I would like to write to this lad in prison and thank him. After all he's been through to think of helping someone else is amazing. I think what you're doing to help keep these ADHD boys out of prison is amazing too."

Mum, 15-year-old ADHD boy

Sarah, I don't know if you remember my son we came to you when he had just moved school to do his A levels... Well, I just wanted to let you know that he got THREE A's today!! The identification by you that he had ADHD (inattentive subtype) was a turning point and I have no doubt that had we never come to you, he would never have got these results. The Ritalin allowed him to focus, together with him loving his subjects, the quality of teaching and their ability to build his confidence and belief that he was very capable has all contributed. He has worked very hard these past two years and it is paid off. Thankyou ! He has got into the University of his choice to do the subject of his choice. To say we are all thrilled and thankful is an understatement.

Mum, 18-year-old boy

So many families like ours have been helped by you and your love and support.

Mum of 3, All ADHD, Herts

I first met sarah in a (YOI) Young offenders' institute. After a couple of failed attempts at counselling they introduced me to her and I am so thankful they did. She was the first person I found I could talk to and be myself.

She was the first person ever to help me to understand that there was reasons for my actions. The first person to ask me how I felt about my mistakes and if I could, what would I change.

She was also the first person to make me realise that it wasn't too late to have a life, and not just 'get by' but a life that I could be proud of, something that I could build and be proud of.

Despite the fact the prison tried to keep us apart, she kept contact, wrote to me at every prison I was moved to half way across the country. She visited me at every opportunity she had and kept me calm every time I got angry or could not cope.

Since prison, Sarah has helped me in almost every aspect of my life - she has helped me more than anyone in my life.

Every part of my life since release has been hard till Sarah stepped in. I was just barely keeping myself afloat till she first helped me with a place to live (temporary accommodation and since she has found me somewhere permanent) then set me up a job so I could work.

Then on top of all that she has now helped me set up in business for myself, got me my ADHD diagnosis, I'm now medicated and confident that in fact I do have a future.

I met Sarah when I was 21 I am now 28. She is the person who changed my life, the only one to understand, my friend and now I consider her my family.

And above all else the only reason why going to prison was one of best things that happened to me.

If I hadn't have met Sarah I would be back in prison or dead by now. And that is a guarantee.

Ex Young Offender, 28, Bucks

BEFORE WE GET GOING

A WORD FROM THE AUTHOR

Hello.

Welcome to what is hopefully the start of you really understanding just what is going on in your ADHD kids' brain. I'm Sarah. I'm a qualified counsellor with an additional qualification in CBT and also a life coach. My aim with this book is to give you insider knowledge on how to be your child's own ADHD therapist together with a THOROUGH understanding of ADHD. My guess is most of us know it is about impulsivity, distraction, inattention, and hyperactivity. But how many know about the hundreds of other traits, thoughts and feelings that go alongside ADHD? I certainly knew barely any of them until 2015.

Then, after half-a-century of exhausting myself, setting up businesses, buying and selling houses and cars, having more ideas per second than most people have in a day, I was finally pounced on by the fifth counsellor I'd seen who said "has anyone ever suggested you have ADHD?"

I looked at her with raised eyebrows. Wasn't ADHD all about nine-year-old boys chucking chairs at teachers? I was a middle-aged counsellor, owner of a highly successful nanny agency and in a 10-year marriage. "No" I replied. "Well, I think you are" she retorted "so go home and Google it".

I did, and in one evening of increasingly frantic Googling, my entire life suddenly dropped into place. It wasn't just one lightbulb moment. It was hundreds. THIS was why I talked too much and over the top of other people. THIS was why I had this horrid internal motor and could not stop working and volunteering. THIS was why nothing ever felt like it was enough, so I was driven to achieve more and more. But it still wasn't enough. THIS was why relaxing or 'just chilling' was alien to me.

It was also why I was bright, quick and became bored so quickly, but could also be gormless when it came to remembering things, dropping things and breaking things. I'd never been able to work out why I was so good at some things and utterly incompetent at others. So many things about me hadn't made sense until that evening.

After a lot of knockbacks from the ill-informed GP's who told me twice there was "no money in the NHS for adult ADHD" a swift kick up the backside from a private psychiatrist to my GP, and suddenly there WAS money in the NHS! I was referred and diagnosed with Moderate to Severe Combined ADHD within three months.

From that day, in March 2015, my life has revolved around ADHD more than I ever could have imagined. I now counsel and coach children, adolescents and adults, both diagnosed with ADHD and those wondering if they are ADHD. I write articles on ADHD and I'm on the APPG for ADHD at the Houses of Parliament. Plus, I train other counsellors so they can spot ADHD in their therapy rooms.

A recurring reason for people coming to see me is parents' lack of understanding of how their ADHD offspring's brains work. The psychiatrists haven't the time to tell you. The NHS recommends ADHD specific therapy after diagnosis but then can't afford to provide it: after their often hard fought for diagnosis, parents of ADHD kids are just left dangling with no one to answer their questions. And quite often with some extremely challenging behaviour going on at home and not a clue as to how to deal with it.

This is where I come in.

This book aims to give you all the answers to those questions that crop up time after time in my therapy room. How our ADHD different brain wiring gives us a totally different way of seeing things; so subsequently we need different handling to get the best out of us.

I'm going to give you both an insight into how your ADHD offspring feels and behaves the way they do - and most important, the very best way to manage that - using 100s of tried and tested techniques straight from the therapy room.

More than anything, I hope this book helps you have a better understanding of your ADHD child. I hope to give YOU a better relationship, and THEM a happier childhood - lessening, if not completely eradicating, the amount of times you get to the end of your tether screeching "I'm going to bl**dy murder the little sh*t!!".

Sarah Templeton Spring 2021

INTRODUCTION

Oh! Not a long introduction that's going to bore me to death!

No. Don't worry. I will keep this bit short, sweet, and informative. And in easy bite-sized chunks for those of us with short attention spans!

WHO IS THIS BOOK FOR?

Anyone who is raising or working with ADHD kids; whether that's mums, dads, other family members or support workers of any kind. If you are spending ANY time with ADHD children this book will give you an insider's sneaky peek into their brain. It will tell you exactly how their ADHD brain works, how to interact with them successfully and how to get the absolute best out of them in just about every scenario at school and at home. And definitely, DEFINITELY, make you less inclined to garrotte them!

WHY BOTHER READING IT?

Because it can all go horribly wrong if you don't. Seriously, not every ADHD kid is going to start smoking weed at nine, get nicked for stealing by ten and be in juvenile court aged eleven. But that can and does happen. I've worked with these adolescents and seen the heart-breaking results of unmanaged ADHD. I'll introduce you to some of these characters throughout the book - not to scare you to death but to inspire you to never, ever give up trying to understand your ADHD kids better.

Young offender units are packed to the rafters with ADHD boys and girls because nobody took the time to help them use their ADHD to achieve greater things.

So well done YOU for picking up this book. You've already given your offspring a real fighting chance. I'm in your corner. Stick with me and together we will give your ADHD children the absolute best chance there is.

WHY SHOULD YOU LISTEN TO ME?

Because I get it. I really, REALLY, get it. Diagnosed moderate to severe ADHD myself, I'd spent 50 years not knowing I had any 'disorder' at all. Yes, I thought differently, spoke faster, did things the quick way and always seemed out of kilter with normal, dare I say, boring people. But I had zero clue that this was because I had any kind of condition. I had never come into contact with mental health services. Why would I? I honestly believed I was the one getting it right, and everybody else was dragging their heels behind!

Then I began work in the English prison system. Back then, I didn't know I was ADHD. All I knew was that I totally GOT these boys, their low boredom thresholds, their need for thrills and excitement, their loathing of authority and their belief that they were always right. I described the way I bonded with each and every offender who slouched in front of me in a grey prison-issue tracksuit, as 'magical'.

Then came that lightbulb moment. My own diagnosis, and only THEN did I realise I 'got them' because they were all like me -ADHD. On further inspection, I discovered that roughly 50% of the young offenders I was working with had been diagnosed ADHD as children, but the rest had no clue. Just like me. They knew they felt and thought differently to 'normal people' but were perplexed as to why.

Since then I have worked with thousands of young offenders and adolescent ADHD kids who have been getting into trouble with the law. I recognise their strong drive for excitement and adrenaline and can understand all that and still respect them. I encourage them to see that they CAN have all the excitement they need without any involvement in drugs, alcohol or crime, and now I'm proud to say I count many of Britain's young offenders as some of my best friends.

It is my deepest joy when I turn another ADHD youngster away from the court and prison system and give them back their freedom and the right to choose the life they want.

But before it gets to this point, it all starts back in the home. Which is why I have written this book. The more you understand your child's ADHD brain, the less they are going to have to kick against. Work WITH your child. Not against them. The more understanding and support they have from you, with the help of this book, the less likely you are to find yourself up in front of any judge. Your ADHD kid needs to know that you are on their side. That you are doing your damnedest to understand them and together you can not only get to grips with their ADHD, but also put them on the path to a hugely successful life.

SO HOW WILL THIS BOOK HELP?

I'm going to break it down for you. There will be no sweeping generalisations. I'll be going into every ADHD trait and idiosyncrasy, most of which I have myself and all of which I have worked with over the years.

The book is structured in such a way that you can dip in and out, just reading the bits that relate to your particular ADHD kids or, for the brave, you can go from start to finish. There are places for notes and a summary at the end of each section so if you're literally at screaming point and need a one sentence refresher, you can grab the book (preferably before you grab their throat!) and have an immediate answer as to how you should handle the current situation as it is happening.

Good luck! I truly wish you all the very best. And remember. Your own ADHD child/children are lucky to have you. Why? Because by picking up this book you've already shown you are trying to understand them. That's huge for your child. So give yourself a pat on the back and let's get started.

REALLY IMPORTANT STUFF
DO READ THIS BIT

WHY IT'S IMPORTANT WE GET YOU SORTED OUT FIRST

Hey! What?

I bet a good many of you are thinking just this while flicking back to the front cover to see if you've picked up the wrong book. Isn't this book about how to help my ADHD child? What's that got to do with me? Well let me enlighten you.

If you have given birth to or fathered one or more ADHD poppets there is a jolly good chance, more than 85% ish at the last reckoning, that you too have ADHD. It is now accepted that ADHD is as inheritable as eye colour and height.

Before you throw the book back on the coffee table and flick the telly on instead, listen up. ADHD IS (nearly always) GENETIC so the chance of one of the offspring's parents having it too is HIGH. In my experience very, very high. It is also possible both parents may have it because - and here is another gem - ADHD adults are often attracted to each other. So, before we go any further, grab your phone and check yourself out with the simple online test at, www.psychcentral.com and in less than ten minutes you will have a strong idea if you're also ADHD and if you score highly enough, I recommend you book yourself in for a swift ADHD assessment - and I'll tell you why.

How you interact with your ADHD child will be affected hugely by whether you are ADHD or not. Just because your ten-year-old is punching walls and kicking his brother, and you wouldn't DREAM of such behaviour, doesn't necessarily mean you aren't ADHD yourself.

I can't begin to tell you the hundreds of ADHD parent clients I've worked with who have casually mentioned "well I've never been able to sit still and have always been a terrible sleeper/an over thinker/a compulsive drinker but I've never been as bad as HIM". Well, I have news for you. ADHD is genetic. But the severity and impact of it ISN'T. So, your teenage tearaway may well be exhibiting off-the-scale appalling behaviour, the like of which you would never dream of doing yourself, but that does not necessarily mean you are not also ADHD.

I have also lost count of the number of parents who think that just because their child is 'just like me so they can't have ADHD'; when, in fact, the parents are as ADHD as the child.

If you can't immediately spot where your child's ADHD has come from look back into the family –

· Did anyone have addiction problems?

· Were any workaholics?

· Were any regularly in and out of prison?

· Were any always angry / violent?

· Were any very overweight?

Chances are higher it is these family members who have undiagnosed ADHD.

It will also help the younger ADHD members of the family not feel so alone with their issues if they know Mum/Dad/Brother/Aunt Flo are also ADHD tribe members, so it is well worth finding out where that ADHD has come from.

Let's work out who else in the household has ADHD first. Then we can move on.

THE THREE DIFFERENT TYPES OF ADHD

I find it incredibly strange that more and more psychiatrists are diagnosing both children and adults purely as 'ADHD' without going into any detail of which variation of the condition they have.

When I was diagnosed back in early 2015, I was told which type and its severity. This was common in those days. You were told whether you had Hyperactive/Impulsive ADHD, Inattentive ADHD or Combined, which is a combination of the two. You were told also whether your ADHD was mild, mild to moderate, moderate, moderate to severe or severe. I don't know why they stopped diagnosing this way, but more and more clients now are coming in to therapy with a diagnosis of ADHD plain and simple. This really is not helpful to either the child with the condition, or their parents and family. There is such a huge difference in the types and varying severity of them, and the first thing you really need to do is work out which category your child falls into. If your child's psychiatrist has been a bit sketchy with the info – read on.

Hyperactive/Impulsive ADHD. This category was applied traditionally to boys: and means you have far too much energy and do things very impulsively. If you think about nine-year-old boys who are constantly fighting, tearing about, have grazes on their knees, get stuck up trees and throw chairs at teachers - this is your archetypal hyperactive ADHD child. They are also typically loud, talkative, argumentative, think they know best about everything, very fidgety, unable to sit still and are generally demanding.

The polar opposite of this is Inattentive ADHD which traditionally was thought to affect girls mainly. If you think back to school, there was usually one girl in every class who was the daydreamer, the one who always seemed to be away with the fairies. She was terribly sweet and kind and everybody liked her, but she was known for being in her own world. This is your traditional Inattentive ADHD child. These kids share a lot of traits with the hyperactive and combined category, but most often they don't show it. Thus, their hyperactivity is often all in their brains. They still have busy brains with lots of thoughts, but they don't show them or put them into action like the other two categories. Those with Inattentive ADHD usually struggle hugely with a lack of motivation and chronic procrastination. They have a lot of ideas which are very rarely put into practice because they don't have the motivation to do that. They tend to end up feeling like underachievers because they've had plenty of ideas, hopes and dreams but very seldom fulfil them. Those with this kind of ADHD usually present as very quiet. They don't speak a lot, especially in groups. They come across as calm and sensible, but inside their brains it is a different matter. They suffer with distraction a lot as well and focus is a real problem for them.

Then you've got the biggest category of all. And this is the one I am in. The 'Combineds'. This group, as I always say, have got it all going on! We are hyperactive, have racing brains, can't sit still, are always on the go, always wanting the next thing, say and do things impulsively and can be quite obnoxious! But we also suffer with distraction, inattention, brain fog and a degree of lack of motivation, along with procrastination when it comes to things which are boring or dull and don't stimulate our brains. As time has moved on, we now know boys can have Inattentive ADHD – and it is now reasonably commonplace. Girls can have purely Hyperactive / Impulsive ADHD – but much less so in my experience.

Parenting these different types of ADHD quite obviously needs to be different. If you have an Inattentive child, it is their lack of motivation and procrastination and their inability to focus and concentrate that's going to give you the biggest problems. If you have a Hyperactive/Impulsive or Combined child you're going to have to deal with most of those traits but also an incredible restlessness; always wanting to move, always wanting to do the next thing and usually more attitude and anger.

The severity of the impact on them also matters hugely. If you have a child with mild or mild to moderate traits you aren't going to have too much to deal with. Probably, lack of concentration at school will be a problem and you might find them difficult to motivate because of procrastination. But you also probably won't be dealing with an awful lot of the other traits people diagnosed moderate or severe will be displaying. It is the moderate to severe and severely impacted ADHD people who really struggle at school and in life. Their traits impact them to the point that life becomes difficult and your parenting skills need to ramp up to deal with it.

Worry not. Help is at hand in this book!

MAKE SURE YOU DO . . . know which ADHD your child has. It is critical for your understanding of their brain.

DON'T EVEN THINK ABOUT. . . assuming all people with ADHD are the same – that couldn't be further from the truth.

THE ADHD TRAITS NOBODY TOLD YOU ABOUT

Read this bit BEFORE you go further, as this section alone might help you understand why your child thinks/does/says SO MUCH stuff that press your buttons.

ADHD isn't all about inattention, distraction, impulsivity and hyperactivity. In fact, that's only a very small part of ADHD in my view. It is these traits HERE that will have a daily impact on your home life, but once you understand this is how your child's brain works - dealing with and managing their behaviour will become a whole lot easier. So, deep breath, and prepare to learn.

ADDICTION. ADHD people are at a much higher risk of developing addiction issues. And we aren't just talking alcohol and drugs - although they often feature heavily in undiagnosed adults. The ADHD brain loves excitement, the buzz, adrenaline and when it GETS it, it LIKES it SO MUCH it wants more! Look out for signs of this in your ADHD child. Addiction can start young. But is not to be confused with fixation. More on that later.

The ADHD brain loves sweet things so if cakes, biscuits, chocolate, or sweeties start disappearing from your cupboards, and your child's waistline is expanding at the same time, you can be pretty sure a sugar addiction is on the way.

ADHD brains are also compulsive. As well as impulsive. So, once the brain gets a taste for that yummy sweetness it is going to want more, and more, and more!

Other addictive behaviour often seen in ADHD kids is gaming, shopping, gambling and, especially with boys, cannabis smoking.

ADRENALINE JUNKIES. The ADHD brain craves adrenaline. Because in simple non-scientific terms (I couldn't stand my science teacher - you'll see the relevance of that later) the brain doesn't have enough dopamine which is the pleasure 'everything's enough' hormone. So, in the ADHD brain, there's just not enough excitement going on. This is why your 8-year old may have flung himself off your garage roof. Or climbed a tree so high he got stuck. He will be doing it, unknowingly, for the buzz. Feeding his adrenaline-seeking brain.

ALWAYS KNOWING BEST. This is one of the traits that causes the most trouble. We do always think we know best. My theory on this is that our brains work quicker than neurotypicals, so we can usually think of a quicker, easier way of doing things. We can't see any reason why anyone else wouldn't want things done our way too...

BEST IN A CRISIS. This is an interesting trait. When there is a crisis such as a car accident, it is the ADHD person who will react quickest and most calmly. And that's because when ADHD brains get flooded with adrenaline they can focus, concentrate and take action much more swiftly than when things are 'normal'. That's why ADHD adults make fantastic paramedics.

NOT THINKING OF THE CONSEQUENCE. ADHD brains don't have the ability to do this. And it is one of the main reasons young offender units are packed with ADHD teens. I'll give you an example of how severe this trait is. I was trying stimulant meds for the first time and threw my house keys down on the edge of a small table. I glanced back at them and thought "don't leave them there, if they fall down the back you won't know where they've gone". I then stood rooted to the spot. In shock. Proper shock. I realised that was the FIRST TIME I had EVER thought of a consequence. Of anything. In over half a century! I'd had no idea before this that my brain wasn't giving a thought to any consequence. Ever. Give this trait a lot of thought. It is a serious issue for ADHD kids. When you want to scream at them 'WHY in Gods name didn't you THINK before you ...(insert any number of careless, hapless, dangerous activities)". Their answer should be "because my brain didn't think of the consequence". It won't be. Because they won't be aware of it. It is up to you to understand this and work with them to 'think before they speak/act' because there's little hope of it happening naturally.

CLEANLINESS. Or lack of. Most ADHD kids go through a patch of not wanting to have a shower or a bath. Or wanting to clean their teeth. I certainly did. I remember going to the dentist once and having to have four fillings because I had decided that cleaning my teeth was way too boring so I'd given it up several weeks before. Around the same age, 12-ish, I decided that bathing was also a waste of my valuable time, so I used to run a bath, sit next to it on a stool reading my book and swishing my fingers in the water every few minutes to fool my mother. I've even met ADHD adults who can't be bothered with the whole 'cleaning yourself' palaver, so if your kid goes through this anti-washing period, do not be surprised.

CLUMSINESS. ADHD kids are usually clumsy. And this often carries through to adulthood. We drop things, break things and damage things on a regular basis. This is caused by a combo of doing things too quickly, not concentrating, getting distracted and being inattentive. "If anyone's going to knock it over, it'll be you" regularly rang in my ears when I was young and had yet again collided with a mug of tea nestling by someone's ankles.

COMPASSIONATE. This is much less known about ADHD but very true. We have more compassion than most. It is why so many ADHD adults give their time up volunteering or working with people/animals in need. We care. Usually deeply. And seeing suffering hurts us.

COMPULSIVITY. The ADHD brain is very powerful. If it finds something it likes - from biscuits to bungee jumping - it is going to demand more and more. And it won't let you stop. Ask any ADHD person if they can stop at one of anything. The likelihood is they can't.

EMOTIONAL DYSREGULATION. Now here's a biggie. In simple terms this means we can't regulate our emotions. Because the executive function part of the ADHD brain that controls emotions doesn't work. What this actually means is an ADHD person's emotions can be all over the place. We can be literally feeling perfectly happy one moment, then a wave of misery can sweep over us. Then ten minutes later be happy as Larry again. This is confusing for parents and siblings. But even more unnerving for the person going through it.

To give you an idea of how impactful this trait is - in the last few years it is been agreed by psychiatrists in the field that the biggest impact of ADHD on someone is not the hyperactivity, distraction, impulsivity, or inattention. It is the emotional dysregulation, an inability to react appropriately to emotions.

ADHD people can't regulate their emotions. They will laugh at funerals or cry at TV adverts. They will often get called 'over sensitive'. Or 'drama queen'. Any ADHD person you talk to will admit this is one of the most difficult aspects of the condition.

EXCESSIVE TALKING & TALKING OVER PEOPLE. This one makes us very unpopular! Whilst Inattentive ADHD people are often quiet and withdrawn, your Combineds and Hyperactives rarely shut up! Our brains are going full speed and we can't get the info out of our mouths quick enough.

ADHD people speak over others and interrupt primarily because if they don't say their thought immediately, it'll be forgotten. Our short-term memory is so poor, we can't hold a thought long enough for you to finish speaking.

FIXATIONS. Once the ADHD brain has found something it likes, it can get extremely fixated or obsessed with it. With children this is often one toy, one teddy, or one doll. As they get older it can be one computer game, one sport or one girl/boy. With an ADHD brain. it is all or nothing We either LOVE something with a passion. Or it is boring and we are over it!

HEIGHTENED SENSE OF JUSTICE. Another unusual one. But this will explain why your kid is often heard wailing "but it is not fair". This would seem to be a bit of a contradiction. After all, aren't ADHD peeps the ones who break rules and loathe authority? Yep. But those same people have a very strong sense of what is right and fair. We hate injustice, discrimination, being ripped off or anyone being taken advantage of. And we won't keep quiet about it.

HYPER FOCUS. Generally thought to be when the normally chaotic and busy brain finds something it really likes. So much so, it banishes all the cluttered thinking, enabling it to concentrate solely on this one exciting new thing. For example, a new interest, like rugby. An ADHD kid won't do anything by halves. If they've decided rugby is their new 'thing' they will eat, sleep and breathe it. They will want every piece of new kit, beg to be taken to rugby matches, be YouTubing it till all hours and admonish you 'for ruining their life' if you refuse to sign them up to a pricey rugby academy. Then, when they've whinged about it till your ears bleed, they'll get bored and decide football is much more their thing!

DIFFICULTY INTERPRETING INSTRUCTIONS & DIRECTIONS. This is a much lesser-known trait but one that has a big impact - especially at school. ADHD brains see/take things differently, and this includes how they interpret instructions and directions from teachers. Sometimes we just haven't got a clue what the teacher actually MEANS until we see somebody else doing it. Your child might not even know this is a problem. Throughout my school years I certainly didn't. But I did know that I often had to glance over the shoulder of the person sitting next to me to understand what the teacher meant. As soon as I glimpsed them starting the work, I knew what I was supposed to be doing. Be very careful about this one because if your child is angry, rude or refusing to do work at school this COULD be the reason behind it.

LABELS IN CLOTHES. Ask the next person you meet to show you the back of their jumper. If the label's been snipped, or torn off in anger, odds are that's an ADHD person who cannot STAND the itchiness of labels. The first thing I do when I arrive home from shopping is grab the scissors and cut out every label, washing instructions and those especially annoying hanger loops! Even the thought of labels is making me itch.

LOSING THINGS. This is one of the biggest frustrations both for and with ADHD kids. From school jumpers to pens, PE kits to text books, and at home - the TV remote! We just cannot find ANYTHING. And I can tell you why. It is because we can't remember where we put it. And why is that? The first ADHD psychiatrist I ever met told me this gem. "For a thought to be stored as a memory, it has to be thought for so many millionths of a second. And an ADHD brain often doesn't do this". So, we literally don't think the thought "I'm putting the remote on the arm of the sofa" long enough for it to become a memory. So have patience with your kids on this one. They'll need visual reminders of where things are. By the way a great tip for the remote is to tie a brightly coloured ribbon round it.

LYING. Why do ADHD kids lie? Not all of them do. But a big chunk do. And I include myself in that. I started lying around 12-ish. Nothing criminal, apart from the odd swipe of chocolate from the newsagent. It was more to do with spicing up my life. One classic was when I'd been late into school after a GP visit. I was later back than expected so told the whole class it was because a male patient had dropped dead in the waiting room. Lord knows why I chose that. And I was found out later the very same day when someone mentioned it to my mother.

There are different theories on why ADHD kids lie. My own is that it makes life more dramatic and therefore interesting. And we do hate boring! Also, we have very poor short-term memory, so sometimes what we genuinely think is the truth, actually isn't. Then there's the need for thrills and excitement. I remember vividly scrawling swear words all over my library book aged about 13. My mother hauled me in front of the chief librarian to apologise - indignant that it WAS NOT ME and berated the librarian, who really should have taken MUCH MORE CARE before releasing books with this FILTH all over them. I remember that poor woman's blushing face to this day - and I still feel guilty.

MELTDOWNS. I bet some of you have come to this section first! The clever people will tell you (probably the ones who liked their science teacher) that meltdowns are because the brain gets overloaded with emotion and doesn't know how to cope. I will tell you that ADHD meltdowns are usually because the child is feeling frustrated, angry, not understood, that something isn't fair or a multitude of other reasons why things are not going their way.

MUDDLING WORDS UP. This is a less known trait but one that seems to affect us all. Our brain doesn't seem to be able to recall the actual word we want. So, for example I will often use the word 'cushion' when I mean 'pillow' Or the word 'glass' when I mean 'window'.

NO RESPECT FOR AUTHORITY. Here we go! This is a humdinger of a trait - it is the one that gets boys locked up in prison and the one that gets us into trouble at school. And as we get older it is the one that gets us into trouble at work. It is also the reason why a massive percentage of adult ADHD people are self-employed. Because, put simply, we do not like being told what to do! There is a caveat here. If we respect somebody, for example a teacher (and nearly always this is because they treat us with respect) we will normally be putty in their hands. But anybody who talks down to us, who is overly authoritative or tells us what to do in anything other than a kind and encouraging manner, beware. It presses the wrong buttons in us and you'll often get a verbal, or even physical, negative reaction.

NOTHING EVER BEING ENOUGH. We have the ADHD brain to thank for this one as well. It is that lack of dopamine which means we are never satisfied - whatever it is we are doing it is usually not enough. The ADHD brain always wants more. More food, more drink, to stay up later, to stay on a computer game longer. It is never satisfied and always wants more.

OVERWHELM. This is a very unknown trait but every ADHD adult you talk to will know this plays a big part in how they feel at times. And ADHD kids have it too. They just won't know how to name the feeling. ADHD brains are unusual in that they can go from feeling 'everything is okay' one minute to being 'totally overwhelmed' the next without any gradual build-up. Thankfully the converse is true and the intense feeling of overwhelm and not being able to cope, can pass just as quickly. But it is debilitating and the effect of it shouldn't be underestimated. I've sold off properties at great financial loss because the feelings of overwhelm were too much to bear.

POOR CONCEPT OF TIME. this is a strange one but one that everybody with ADHD has. We have a very poor concept of ALL time. That includes time in the past, the present and the future. In the past we find it very difficult to know how long ago something was. A simple question like "when did you last do any maths homework" is likely to be met by a blank face and an "I don't know". This is not your child being deliberately vague. They probably have no clue.

Time issues in the present mean we are very poor judges of how long something is going to take. Neurotypical kids can work out that tidying up their room, packing their schoolbag and having a shower before tea will take 40 minutes. The ADHD kid will tell you 15. And mean it. I was shocked to find out only recently I had a reputation for being late. Then I realised I had hardly any idea how to work out how long anything was going to take. It is always just a random guess.

PROCRASTINATION. Now this is a huge one. And very probably the trait that could potentially be giving you more problems at home with your child than any other. Procrastination is a strange one when it comes to ADHD. Those of us who are combined or hyperactive often don't have much trouble with it. Our problem is more often not being able to do things quickly enough. But people with Inattentive ADHD and Combined ADHD who are high on the inattentive side, can have absolutely colossal problems with procrastination. Procrastination is the reason also why people with ADHD are often called 'lazy'. They are far from it actually, but it can present as chronic laziness.

It is an executive malfunction in the ADHD brain that is responsible for procrastination problems. You might have heard the expression 'brain fog'. A lot of people with ADHD describe their brain as if it is 'surrounded by thick cotton wool' or doing anything at all is 'like walking through treacle' and they can't get it to move or function in any way. A lot of ADHD people know exactly what needs doing and how to do it, but they cannot get their brain to propel them into doing it. This goes for adults too. Medication can help hugely with procrastination, but until your child is on the right dose of the right medication you may find their procrastination and inability to 'just get on with things', will drive you round the twist.

The scientific explanation for this is that an ADHD brain will only get motivated by something it finds exciting. So, you can bet our life if you are offering pizza, chips and ice cream your child won't find it hard to find the motivation to sit at the dinner table. It is when you're asking them to do their homework that the procrastination will kick in. It is really not them being difficult, although this is how it will seem. The brain is a powerful driver and unless there is excitement and adrenaline involved, an ADHD brain will put off doing whatever is dull and repetitive or lacking in excitement.

PUSHING BOUNDARIES. This is a trait that has a very big impact, especially on teenagers. It goes along with 'thinking we know best' and 'wanting things our own way'. ADHD people on the whole have very little respect for boundaries and want to push against all of them. Ironically ADHD kids AND adults work better in a structured environment, but expect your child to kick against boundaries. Our brain just doesn't like being told what to do.

REJECTION SENSITIVE DYSPHORIA (RSD). This is something very few people know about, but it will almost definitely have a huge impact on your child, especially when they hit puberty. Rejection Sensitive Dysphoria quite literally means an out of proportion, over sensitivity to rejection. In literal terms this will mean that your child is very sensitive to rejection, in particular humiliation or criticism. And they will often react to rejection with anger, either verbal or physical. RSD also means an ADHD brain will perceive rejection when it is not really there. Perceived rejection can be as cripplingly painful as actual rejection. Their reaction to it often leads them to be called 'drama queens' or 'overly sensitive' and accusations of 'always wanting to be the centre of attention'

RISK TAKING & THRILL SEEKING. This is a trait that can often take ADHD people in one of two directions. The need for adrenaline and excitement can mean a lot of ADHD people engage in extreme sports such as bungee jumping and paragliding. Sport is a very good way to satisfy the brain's need for adrenaline. Popular and more accessible are non-team sports like running, cycling and boxing. The other direction is not so good and one which you need to keep a close eye on. Often by early teens boys, in particular, are looking for more risky and exciting activities. This can be smoking weed/cigarettes, trying alcohol, and before long can lead to them mixing with older boys who are 'more exciting' than their own age group. These boys will often get them involved in petty crime - and before you know it you've got a 13-year-old who is drinking, smoking and in trouble with the law.

SENSORY ISSUES. Whilst more common with ASD (Autistic Spectrum Disorder), ADHD children often have their fair share of sensory issues. These can be far reaching. Some ADHD kids will have problems with food, for example having to have things served up in different bowls so food isn't touching. Or only eating with their hands. Others will have issues with material they will wear. I remember vividly as a teenager hating anything that was nylon, wool or itchy. I've noticed a lot of ADHD people only wear cotton, jersey and denim.

Noise is another problem. A lot of ADHD people are extremely sensitive to loud noise, for example in restaurants. I've met ADHD people who don't like to be touched and others who have issues around certain smells. All the senses can be affected by ADHD and this is one that varies hugely person to person. There is no norm.

STEALING. There are a lot of ADHD traits that tap into this one. I certainly used to steal as a teenager and most clients I work with did as well. Luckily, for most of us, this tails off as we get near adulthood and realise that we don't fancy a criminal record. But.....

ADHD kids and young teenagers will almost certainly steal at some point. For most it starts with taking money from Mum's purse. The more serious will then progress to swiping your credit card details or sneakily visiting the ATM with your debit card. Mostly this is the need for the adrenaline and excitement stealing things brings. But there is an also an element of our compulsive shopping and wanting bright, new and shiny things. Also, if an ADHD person wants something, they want it now! Right now! Saving up for things isn't exciting so they will very often take the money or steal the item because having it NOW is crucial.

SLEEP PROBLEMS. This can go one of two ways. Most ADHD people have trouble sleeping and this can start right from birth. Mums report ADHD babies wanting little sleep and keeping them up all night. ADHD children often have trouble switching off at night, waking up during the night or waking up too early. On the whole, ADHD people need less sleep than others. Inattentive ADHD people usually however report the opposite. They can sleep like logs and many feel they sleep far too much.

WANTING TO WIN/BE FIRST. Again, a lesser-known trait but one that applies pretty much across the board with ADHD. One of my clients told me that "coming second was in effect losing" and I have to agree with him. We do like to win and come first which probably explains why so many top athletes and sports people are ADHD.

DON'T EVEN THINK ABOUT . . . assuming its only hyperactivity / distraction / inattention / impulsivity that constitutes your child's ADHD and the rest of their behaviour is them being a 'little git'. There are so many other ADHD traits.

WHAT WORKS BETTER . . . having a real understanding of ALL the traits that apply to your child.

REWARD SYSTEMS AND WHY THEY ARE
YOUR NEW BEST FRIEND

If you only read one chapter in this book, make it this one. Reward systems could literally change your life. First of all, let me explain what's going on in your ADHD kid's brain ...

ADHD brains are under-stimulated. They need excitement, adrenaline or a reward to get them to engage. If it is not exciting or doesn't involve food or pleasure your child's ADHD brain is just not going to be very interested. However, there is one very simple way of getting their brain to show interest. And that is by giving it something it WANTS. Something exciting. Something that will give it adrenaline! And this is where reward systems come in.

Reward systems are your secret weapon. They don't need to be used just ad hoc. They can be used in every area of your ADHD kid's life. Your child's brain is like this 24/7. And the way to get their brain motivated is most definitely by rewarding it. I cannot stress this enough. It is not your child being wilfully difficult and not wanting to do boring things – it is the ADHD brain. Once you get this into your head and understand that if you work with your child's brain rather than against it your life is going to be a whole lot easier. Reward systems can range from the intricate and grandiose to the incredibly simple.

A simple example would be exactly what I'm doing now. I'm writing this chapter before telling myself I can have anything to eat. See I'm 57 and still use my own reward systems to get me to do things. I can do that because I understand how my brain works and I can set up my own reward systems. I do it all the time. Probably every day.

It is the way I get things done. But your child isn't going to realise this is how their brain works, so YOU are going to need to put the reward systems in place. If you haven't used reward systems before then I strongly recommend you sit down and have a really good think about what it is that excites your child. I'm going to guess it is some of these things ~

- More time on the Xbox / Playstation

- Going to bed slightly later

- Not having to do the washing up or empty the dishwasher or any other chore that bores them

- Having the iPad for an extra half hour in the evening

- Extra money to buy clothes or trainers

- Tickets to see their favourite football team or band

- Choosing which takeaway the family have on a Saturday night

- Extra pocket money

- Having friends round for a sleepover

- Choosing a theme park day out

- Choosing which food goes into a picnic

- Picking which ice cream flavours get bought this month

- The chance to go to TGI Friday's or Nando's

Before you think about putting any reward system in place, first of all spend a good couple of weeks thinking about ALL the things that motivate and excite your child. It really doesn't matter what it is. But you'll be able to identify these things because they will be the things that your particular child will have never given you any grief over! Another simple example is beans on toast. I loved beans on toast as a child but didn't have it very often. For me it was a massive treat. I also loved it when we had what I called 'a buffet tea'. Something where I could pick lots of bits. Both of these things would've been enough to get me motivated enough to do something boring beforehand. So, think hard here – the more you come up with, the more successful you'll be.

The next step is identifying areas where you want your child's behaviour to change. I don't have to give you examples of this. I'm quite sure you know exactly what it is you struggle with getting your child to do. From homework to brushing their teeth to tidying their room ... your list could be quite extensive!

So next we have to put the reward system in place. There are some golden rules with reward systems so before we start you need to have a good grasp of them ~

- The reward system has to be maintained. Don't ever start something you can't keep going. For example, don't promise football tickets every month if it is going to bankrupt you.

- It has to be clearly communicated to everybody involved. For example, it is no good you knowing the system and their dad not. Everybody needs to be completely up to speed on what the expectations are and what the rewards are. Especially if the father lives in one house and mother in another.

- There needs to be short-term goals and long-term goals. Your child is going to get bored if there is no reward within a week. A week is the absolute maximum you should push it without them getting some sort of recompense.

- The expectations and rewards need to be visual. Remember your child won't be able to hold the information in their head. So, you need to get yourself a nice big whiteboard, a blackboard or some vibrant coloured pens and nice paper. It needs to be SEEN and it needs to be in your child's mind all the time.

- It needs to be collaborative. It is no good you deciding what the reward is going to be if your child isn't interested. You can come up with the suggestions, but they have to be agreed by them. It is the only way it will work.

• It needs to be accumulative so for example if they meet your behavioural expectations for seven days, there needs to be an extra reward for completing a full week. Your child will soon get bored if they do something for seven days solid and there is no reward for maintaining that long.

• There must be enough benefit in it for you. If you get the balance wrong and it is all about rewards and you're not seeing much change in their behaviour, you are soon going to become resentful.

• The rewards need to be changed, or 'upgraded' as your child needs to see it, on a reasonably regular basis. As soon as their brain is finding something boring/routine they are going to need the rewards ramped up. As an incredibly rough guide I would say every three months.

Now comes the bit where you need to make some decisions. The fact that you are putting rewards in place needs to be introduced to your child at the right time and when they're in the right mood. For example, it is no good doing it when they are in a grump, tired, hungry or having major arguments with somebody in the house. Any suggestion of a reward system at these times is going to be met with hostility. Instead make it a time when you and your child are communicating well; they're in a good mood, laughing or coming to you for a cuddle. Suggest it as AN IDEA. Don't TELL them they've got to do it. Explain in a positive way that you want to reward them when they do things well, and you'd like their help with putting a system in place so they can regularly have nice things. If you present the idea this way, no ADHD child is going to say 'no' Remember their brain wants rewards.

Once you've come up with the rewards, they would like to be included now is the time to broach what you want them to change. Again, this needs very delicate handling. Don't say things like "well you've got to stop doing this" and "you've got to start doing that." This will only put your kid's back up. Instead talk about how they 'struggle' to do certain stuff and you totally understand how boring these things can be. And how you want to make it 'easier' for them. Keep everything positive. Avoid the negatives. Definitely don't tell them off for anything they've been doing; or not doing. Instead assure them you understand this is how their wonderful ADHD brain works and you want to reward them when it does the good stuff.

Once you have your child's acceptance and you've agreed COLLABORATIVELY what it is they are going to change to make their life easier, and what rewards are going to be put in place, you're good to go!

Remember it doesn't all have to be very sophisticated, there can be daily extra rewards like "I've bought some Magnums so if you want to go and just quickly tidy your room we can have them afterwards". Little simple things like this really do work.

Here are some examples of reward systems my clients have put in place for their young children and teenagers. These have WORKED so variations on these could be a very good place for you to start ~

Example 1

An 11-year-old boy hated going to bed. His mum put in place a system whereby if he went to bed by 8 pm having had a shower and making no fuss, beside his bed would be a cookie and a glass of milk. If he did this for the five days during the week he was allowed to choose the DVD and takeaway the family shared on Saturday evening.

Example 2

A 12-year-old girl was very defiant and wouldn't do anything she was told. The mum put in place a system whereby if she didn't answer back and did as she was asked all week, each Saturday she would be given £15 to spend on clothes. If she managed the whole month of this behaviour, then she was given an extra £50 on the final weekend to spend as she wished.

Example 3

A 13-year-old client hated showering or bathing. The mum was at her wits end because the child really whiffed! They put in a reward system whereby if he had a shower every other day and at least a wash in between (if he couldn't be bothered to shower), he would be given £1 every day. If he managed this for a full week, he was given an additional £10 on Saturday to spend on anything he wanted.

Example 4

There was a very long list a 14-year-old client of mine wouldn't do. He fought against doing homework, showering, was swearing prolifically at his family and having physical fights with his sister. The mum put in individual reward systems for each behavioural change she wanted. It ranged from 50p a day for not swearing at all and a £1 for every day he didn't fight with his sister. He liked it because he saw lots of different ways to make money. There were a lot of blips but on the whole the behaviour changed.

Example 5

A 15-year-old girl found it very hard to motivate herself to do anything. She was incredibly bright but really struggled to do homework and anything school related. Her mum put in place a reward system whereby she could choose whatever they watched on television between 8 pm and 9 pm as long as she had finished her homework before. If she managed this for a full week, she could have the roast of her choice on Sunday with a DVD of her choice. This girl had a particular love of roast dinners!

Hopefully reading these has given you some ideas for what might work for your ADHD child. Always remember ALL decisions have to be collaborative. It just won't work if they aren't.

DON'T EVEN THINK ABOUT . . . underestimating the power of reward systems. They could completely change how your child functions at home.

WHAT WORKS BETTER . . . give a lot of thought as to what it is motivates your child and what behaviour it is you want them to change. Take time in putting reward systems in place and you will reap the benefits.

What worked and what didn't?

WHEN THEY WON'T DO AS THEY'RE TOLD

This will come as a shock, but there will come a day when your perfectly behaved cherub will suddenly rebel and you'll be speechless when they resolutely refuse to do whatever it is you've just asked of them.

In fact, you'll be so shocked, I guarantee you'll ask them to do it several times more, yet there isn't even a slim chance of it happening.

Your child hasn't suddenly been replaced overnight by a demon child, but their ADHD HAS just kicked in! There are lots of traits that feed into this 'not wanting to be told what to do'. It could be any of the following ADHD traits and most likely a combo of all of them ~

- ✓ Feeling that we know best.
- ✓ Always wanting everything our own way.
- ✓ Not liking being told what to do.
- ✓ Struggling to interpret instructions and directions.
- ✓ Lack of motivation (especially if something is routine or boring).
- ✓ Procrastination (unless it is very exciting with immediate reward).

That's quite a mixture to be going on in any child's ADHD brain and at some stage they are going to rebel and not adhere to whatever you are instructing them to do.

This is particularly difficult for parents. I have my own theory on this. I think it is why ADHD children on the whole get on much better with grandparents and aunties and uncles and often really struggle to get along with parents. If you think about it, it makes complete sense. For a brain that doesn't like being told what to do, the parents are usually the main overseers of discipline, rules, instructions and restrictions.

My own example is pretty typical. I clashed with my mother on a daily basis because it was her who was hands-on in bringing me up. My father, who I only saw part time, was much easier to get along with. Partly I now believe because he was ADHD himself but also because, only seeing him once a week, there was no discipline involved. It was all FUN with dinners out, bowling, swimming, cinema and with my brain being suitably entertained and not controlled, so I was probably easier to have around. It certainly felt easy from my point of view. No constant nagging and boring discipline like at home. It also helped having a stepmother who worked at Mars and brought home selection bags of sweets every week, which I was allowed to eat to my heart's content. No relaxed indulgences ever happened in my own house.

I also had a fantastic relationship with my Nan who never told me what to do, how to behave, how to speak, how to sit, how to eat, or the thousand other things my mother constantly threw at me in a bid to bring me up properly.

This led to a long term, smouldering resentment of my mother. She didn't have the benefit of knowing I was ADHD so treated me like a neurotypical child and I was anything but.

Luckily, you are better informed. You know that your child or children are ADHD, so I can tell you how to get the best out of them.

There are some very cool tricks I have learnt by handling my undiagnosed ADHD niece from when she was one year old. And this works with kids and teens with ADHD without a shadow of a doubt. It is very simple and you might think it is so simple that it isn't worthwhile - but trust me on this. This is crucial information if you want your kids to do as you ask.

1. Ask. Don't tell. If you ask an ADHD child if they would like to have their dinner you are going to get a much better response than if you say "your dinner is on the table - eat it". Instantly, your child's hackles will be up because they are being told what to do. Reframe it as a question and there will be no irritation.

2. Give choices. I've used this one and it works. When my four-year-old niece didn't want her dinner, I gave her three options. One was to eat from a tray on the sofa, the second was to eat at the kitchen table, and the third was to eat at the dining table. She looked at me murderously, knowing she had been caught out but also realising that I had also just put her in charge. I'd sought her opinion, which made her feel important and she therefore made a decision - passing on her wisdom, as she saw it!

3. Negotiate. Your ADHD child will have reasons why they are against doing something. It is up to you to find out what those reasons are. Some may be unreasonable, but some may be just. For example, if your child has social anxiety or any of the other coexisting conditions of ADHD, there may well be a genuine reason why they don't want to do something. So, it is definitely worth opening up the conversation around what it is you want them to do and why they are not keen to do it.

It is going to be a very rare ADHD child who doesn't give you this problem. At its earliest, this trait will kick in from the age of two - but if you're lucky it might not arise till puberty. But trust me, it is going to feature heavily in the teenage years.

Watch the tone of your voice when you speak to an ADHD child. Any sign of anger, irritation, bossiness or unreasonableness will be met with at the very least frostiness and at worst anger and meltdowns. If you keep your voice soft and ASK things, keeping it POSITIVE and QUESTIONING rather than telling - you are always going to get a much better response than somebody who is shouting orders.

When getting your child to do anything becomes a real struggle, you might want to consider a reward system. This 'not wanting to be told what to do' is one of the very best reasons to implement a reward system.

DON'T EVEN THINK ABOUT . . . barking orders, shouting, getting visibly angry when they won't do something or trying to force them into action by screaming louder and losing your temper.

WHAT WORKS BETTER . . . Try to get underneath what is really going on. What is the problem? Why do they not want to do it? Do they have a genuine reason? Or is it time for negotiation, compromise or to put a reward system in place to make sure it happens?

What worked and what didn't?

WHEN THEY ALWAYS WANT TO KNOW WHY?

This is a nice easy one to understand even if this constant questioning has been doing your head in up to now.

It is dead simple. An ADHD brain is inquisitive. It doesn't 'just do it' because you're telling it to do something. It wants to know WHY?! And if you can't give a jolly good reason WHY .... guess what. That ADHD brain is very probably not going to persuade itself it should do it. Whatever 'it' is.

The best example of this trait I can give is mock exams. You know - those 'pretend' exams you have at school before the 'actual' exams! A lovely, placid, and academically bright ADHD girl client of mine (destined for A levels and university) put the fear of God into her parents after taking her mocks, so by the time I met her the family were already in crisis. Daisy, 15, had horrified her teachers by putting her head on her desk and SLEEPING through all her mock exams. The school was furious and perplexed; her parents in full-on panic mode. But within one therapy session, Daisy and I had worked it out.

There was just no point was there? She didn't understand WHY they were important. It suddenly clicked - I had felt EXACTLY the same way at 15! What was the POINT of mocks?! They didn't mean anything. Didn't count towards anything. There was no REWARD for passing them. She didn't understand WHY they mattered. Neither had I. So why bother?

We sorted this one out by giving Daisy her OWN reasons for trying at the next batch of mocks. She would do her best in each subject to gauge for HERSELF how much work she needed to do before the actual exams. It worked! She'd got her reason 'why'.

This is an often-overlooked trait of ADHD. But it is a powerful one and can have a huge bearing on your kid's behaviour. Unless there's a very good reason WHY something should be done, the ADHD brain will struggle to motivate itself to do it.

The other huge point to make here is that until you give your inquisitive ADHD child an answer, they aren't going to let it drop. And believe it or not, this isn't them being difficult on purpose. It is their brain that won't 'let something go' until it can make sense of whatever it is asking. They don't want flannel. They don't want fobbing off. They just want the TRUTH. Right now. Quick. No sugar coating and no hanging around. Give them that and they'll be off and running. Until the next time.

However annoying it is to keep answering the constant WHY question, if you give them the true answer quickly, you'll be surprised how soon they let it drop. And always keep answers positive.

Example.

Child "When is dinner ready mum? I'm starving"

Mum "It's not ready yet honey" (negative)

Child "Oh why? I'm dying of starvation. Why can't we eat now? Why didn't you start earlier? WHY?"

You have just given them a reason for a potential meltdown.

Better if mum had been positive and said, "The veggies are just boiling so it'll be seven minutes and it will be on the table, and it'll be even quicker if you lay the table."

This way her offspring not only knows WHY it is not ready but also has a positive message to cling to, and a part to play in speeding things up. This worked for me as a child.

So have an answer ready for why it is important they get dressed/get off their PlayStation/eat/drink whatever. And make it the truth.

Remember - they genuinely need to know the answer WHY before their brain can let it go and move on.

DON'T EVEN THINK ABOUT . . . ever saying "just because" or "because I said so" or "because I'm your mother and you'll do as I say" in answer to the 'why' question. Recognise it's a genuine need to understand the importance/relevance/reason for something. All you will do, by not giving a quick and truthful answer, is risk a lot of whingeing and moaning and in the worst cases, a fist or foot through the wall/telly as the child gets so frustrated.

WHAT WORKS BETTER . . . always give a reason or an explanation. Don't be vague or noncommittal. When an ADHD person asks you a question they need an answer. And make it a firm one that you stick to!

What worked and what didn't?

WHEN THEY WON'T STOP FIDGETING AND CAN'T SIT STILL

I'm guessing you've worked out the H in ADHD stands for HYPERACTIVITY ... but have you linked that to the fact that your ADHDer is constantly on the move?

This is a proper problem. Not to be taken lightly. We have to keep something moving or we implode. I tried this experiment with a teenage ADHD client once. We challenged each other to sit perfectly still, arms flat on the arm rest of the therapy room chairs. And we'd time how long we could sit. I don't think we made it past 15 seconds. It was literally painful having to do it. Even we were shocked how little time we could sit still.

As a teen and as an adult I was constantly told to sit still, stop shuffling, stop moving and stop fidgeting - in cinemas and theatres particularly. The strange thing was I wasn't even aware that I was doing any of these things. But I must've been because everybody and their dog told me I was annoying them by doing it. This was of course many years before my ADHD diagnosis.

Now I understand that my urge to keep moving is stimulating my brain. And when I stop my brain gets very frustrated and antsy.

So, if your child is driving you nuts by tapping their fingers, fiddling with their hair, shaking a leg or keeping one part of their body constantly moving - now you know why.

Medication helps with this a fair bit, as does having something in your hand to fiddle with. In every therapy session I hold either a fidget toy or a pen and I'm constantly discreetly twirling it in my hand. If I didn't, I would get very anxious and wound up. It really does help to calm you down by having something to fiddle with. And by being calm, hey presto, we can think and concentrate on other things.

So definitely think of getting your child fidget toys, fidget spinners or anything that will keep their hands busy as this will mean they will be able to concentrate and stay calm much more easily.

Also take a lenient view when you are in a restaurant or somewhere else where your child is expected to sit for a long time. It is a much better idea to let them eat and then go off to a play area or go outside with a responsible adult. Asking any ADHD child to sit at a table for a very long time is asking for trouble. Odds are they will be fine while they're eating, but straight after that they will be bored. They will need more stimulation so you either need to bring activities for them to play with at the table or allow them to leave.

ADHD kids, boys in particular, need exercise every day. This really helps give the nervous energy an outlet. It also gives adrenaline which calms their brains. Team sports can cause problems - not always, but often. I've had many a teen client who has been sent off for accusing football or rugby referees of being "totally blind" because they, the teen, know the rules better!

Adrenaline loaded solo sports like running, cycling, swimming and climbing are usually safer. Boxing is also a great discipline and exercise option. I always recommend that teen ADHD boys have a punch ball, punch bag, or swing-ball which they can go and take their inner-restlessness out on.

This is usually best in a place where they can't be watched; maybe a garage, basement, summer house or at least in a room no-one else uses. A good punch will definitely take the excess energy out of your child!

DON'T EVEN THINK ABOUT . . . constantly having a go at them for fidgeting or not sitting still. Remember they really cannot help it.

WHAT WORKS BETTER . . . make sure you've got a ready supply of fidget spinners or fidget toys wherever you go. Check if they can use them at school and make sure they've got them if you're going to the cinema, theatre or restaurant. Take age-appropriate colouring books/toys/devices if you're going anywhere you know your child will be bored.

What worked and what didn't?

WHEN THEY'RE CONSTANTLY MOANING "I'M BORED"

Whichever sort of ADHD you're dealing with I can pretty much guarantee you are going to hear this often "I'm bored!". Don't tell them off for it. An ADHD brain needs a lot of stimulation and the minute it doesn't get it, yes, it IS bored. When you hear them say they are bored, replace the B word in your brain with 'under-stimulated' because that's what they mean. They just don't know that yet. I remember being told the word 'bored' was banned when I was young because I used it so often. And I was always being told to "go and read a book". Which was fine and I did, until I became bored with that too.

This is a very easy one to understand. Your ADHD child's brain needs and craves more stimulation than a normal brain. It is constantly looking for excitement, for something new, for something different and for something challenging. The right medication helps hugely with this and should allow your child's need for 'something more' to calm down. An unmedicated ADHD child however will be forever searching for something new and exciting to do.

There are lots of things you can do to help with this. Daily exercise is a brilliant way for your child to receive the right dose of adrenaline. Unless it is tipping with rain, get your child outdoors and active.

Indoors, always have a ready supply of whatever it is that excites your child's brain. If it is arts and crafts - always have a good supply and introduce new bits every time - it doesn't matter how cheap and cheerful they are, because anything new will count as exciting to your child. It can be literally a different piece of coloured cardboard or a pack of cheap felt pens. An ADHD brain is easily fooled - if it is new, it is exciting.

Try and break up activities, especially during school holidays. It is not good to leave an ADHD child with absolutely nothing to do all day. Make sure there is something scheduled at some point of the day. Whether that's a dog walk, a picnic, a swim, a game of rounders, a cinema visit, whatever it is try and add at least one 'event' into each day, so your ADHD child has something to look forward to and get excited about.

Always be prepared for the 'post activity crash'. It is always very disappointing for an ADHD brain when an activity ends, so make sure when you come home from whatever you've been doing, there is something nice to look forward to. It can be as simple as a bar of chocolate - just give your child something to be 'excited' by when an activity ends. I've known clients to be absolutely bewildered by their child's meltdown when they come home from having had a lovely time out. I can guarantee it is because of this. Once that adrenaline stops pumping, your child is going to get very grumpy if there is nothing nice to look forward to. Picking up fish and chips or another takeaway on the way home is another very good plan.

Above all, your child needs to be kept occupied. For those without social anxiety, sign them up to as many clubs as they are interested in. Encourage them to be active as much as you possibly can.

DON'T EVEN THINK ABOUT . . . telling them it is wrong or irritating or too demanding to keep saying they're bored or shout at them that they CAN'T be bored when you've just come home from an exhausting day entertaining them for eight hours.

WHAT WORKS BETTER . . . understand that this is just their way of saying their brain needs more stimulation. Communicate with them about what it is they want/need to do and encourage creative and sporting activities. Become a frequent visitor to Poundland or other cheap shops, picking up colourful and interesting little bits in the arts and craft and stationery sections. Pre-empt the post activity crash by having something nice lined up for afterwards.

What worked and what didn't?

WHEN THEY THINK THEY KNOW BEST AND WANT EVERYTHING THEIR OWN WAY

This is a biggie. If you have an ADHD child, you'll already know how much this affects your life!

But did you know it is an actual ADHD trait? 'Thinking we know best' and 'Wanting things our own way' is the way our brain is wired. Bearing in mind I wasn't diagnosed ADHD till I was 51, my mother spent decades calling me "a control freak" and saying, "why does everything have to be YOUR way?". Now we know! It is not the easiest trait to have and it does lose us friends. You can imagine how the ADHD child in a group of mates always wanting to do joint activities the way THEY want, would drive the others nuts. It is also not easy with teachers. And definitely not with parents!

How do you handle it? Particularly with pre-teens and teens who haven't yet developed the awareness to know how to tone down this side of their personality.

Firstly. Don't argue. This will get you nowhere. Except into a heated argument, or worse a meltdown. Whatever your ADHDer has just decreed as law, such as the television needs to be this loud / I'm not going to school / we need to get rid of the dog - DO NOT come out with a straight "No. Don't be stupid" type of comment. Instead ask questions.

Yes, you did hear me right. Asking questions in a genuinely inquisitive manner (not sarcastically or patronisingly) will do two things.

1) it will make your child feel important. Remember they like to feel they're in charge, so you are straight away playing into that element of their brain.

2) it will make them feel like their opinion matters. So, they will gladly share their wisdom with you. This will get them talking.

As they start communicating calmly - now is your chance to help them to see things from another angle - yours.

So, here's an example.

> ADHD "I hate the dog. Get rid of it."
> Mum "Really? Ok. What don't you like about him?" (Notice the "OK". Use frequently! It's calming. Shows acceptance)
> ADHD "He woke me up today with his barking."
> Mum "Oh, how annoying. Wasn't he downstairs as usual? "
> ADHD "No. He was outside my bedroom."
> Mum "Oh, we can't have that. How about we lock him in the lounge, so he stays there till morning?"
> ADHD "Ok"

Hey presto. No meltdown. No argument.

See. It's easy! Well, it is if you remember to question rather than tell.

Another thing to bear in mind is that often we DO know best. Why? Because our brain can often see the quicker/easier way of doing something. So, if your ADHDer is proclaiming that something can be done better - give them the chance to explain what and how. Again, ask questions. Give them the opportunity to express what's going on in their brain. Listen. Hear. Discuss. Negotiate. Compromise. Agree - in that order.

And remember that once something has come into an ADHD brain - it has to come out. We can't just put the idea to one side and move on. Our brain won't let us. So, let them speak. Let them get it all out. Then with gentle questioning (with no hint of sarcasm or belittling) discuss whatever it is they're thinking.

ADHD kids will push you. Some push blooming hard. I've seen it in therapy. They have no concept they could be wrong. And no concept that your opinion might be the more reasoned let alone right. Your questioning skills may need brushing up on. Google 'motivational interviewing'. It is handy in situations like this.

Above all, let your ADHD kid know you are on their side. It is you and them against the world. If you can start them young, knowing you are on their team, then issues like this don't impact so much. The more you battle an ADHD child the more aggro you'll have in your life. Their brain is powerful, especially during puberty when their hormones are all over the place. Their strength at wanting their own way could shock you.

DON'T EVEN THINK ABOUT . . . ignoring their views. Don't ridicule or mock them. Don't tell them to "Shut up" or say "NO" without them being given a chance to speak.

WHAT WORKS BETTER . . . ask questions. Listen intently. Take them seriously. Show that you are genuinely interested. Gently encourage them to look at things a different way. Ask if there IS another way of looking at it. Hone your negotiating skills!

What worked and what didn't?

WHEN THEY ANSWER BACK AND ARGUE WITH YOU

This is another very big problem and potentially the reason you bought this book in the first place! Answering back to parents, arguing relentlessly with brothers and sisters and seemingly being able to start a fight in an empty room is an absolute ADHD trait. And there is a very good reason for it.

Before we get to that point. Just a bit of empathy from me to you. It is a very rare ADHD child who doesn't like an argument. This usually starts from the age of about eight or nine. I have seen children as young as five give their parents a right mouthful if they are told off, but generally it is when puberty looms that the problem really starts.

At the very least your child will be deemed to have 'attitude'. I had this levelled at me from the age of about 12. If only I could change my attitude everything would've been okay - apparently! But I couldn't. I wasn't purposely behaving in any way. It was my natural demeanour. But it seemed to offend people deeply. Even my Nan, who I worshipped and adored, told me I made her feel an inch tall when I was about 12. I was mortified as I didn't ever want to hurt her, but this apparently was all down to my attitude.

You might get away with your kid just having this sort of 'screw you' attitude, but often that's not enough for a spiky ADHD teen.

More often they will argue the toss about anything and everything and will leave you exasperated by their seemingly never-ending enthusiasm for an argument.

There are a lot of ADHD traits that feed into this, but first let's talk about the brain. An ADHD brain gets adrenaline from fighting. It loves not only banter but a proper full-on fight and the more you engage or argue back, the more it is going to carry on.

Have you ever bellowed at your ADHD kid that you are sick of them having to have the last word? I can almost guarantee you have. That's because their ADHD brain will not let it go! If you say something to them, they just have to say something back.

So what you need to do is be one step ahead. Remember that their ADHD brain is seeking adrenaline and it can get that from having a good old shouting match with you or anybody else. If your aim is to get the shouting to stop then you've only got to do ONE thing. It is a very simple thing but it is also the hardest to do in the circumstances. That is to say nothing and walk away.

Try it. It is very powerful. If you think it is difficult for you, learn from the young offenders I worked with in prison who I told to walk away from baying crowds - desperate to see them fight. It nearly crippled them doing it the first time, but with practice they could walk away and without exception they all then realised the power they had gained by doing this. That power really is in your hands and if you can walk away, shut the door and move to another room, your child's brain will soon lose interest in fighting as it is not being fed the adrenaline. It is a good idea to tell siblings to do exactly the same. Putting it simply, the more you engage with ADHD fighting talk, the longer you are going to prolong the episode.

A lot of the time you will find this arguing talk is due to the ADHD trait of 'having a heightened sense of justice'. If anything seems to be unfair you can guarantee your ADHD child is going to become outraged. They will go from 0 to 100 in two seconds flat if they feel they are being taken advantage of or things aren't fair.

The other trait at play here is the fact that your child will always 'think they know best' and 'are always right'. Remember this is not a choice. It is the way their brain works.

Something else to be wary of is the fact that your ADHD child's brain won't let something drop. Unlike a neurotypical brain which can just let something go, this never happens in an ADHD brain. If something isn't right or fair or just, the ADHD brain will keep ruminating and overthinking it and will absolutely not be able to let it go.

If this is a really serious problem it might be a good idea to get your child tested for Oppositional Defiant Disorder (ODD) and Pathological Demand Avoidance (PDA). Kids with these conditions take arguing to a higher level. I often wonder now if I would have been diagnosed with Oppositional Defiant Disorder myself - any sign of incompetence and I leap on people from a great height!

Your goal is to get to a position where you're not giving your child anything to shout about. This is a real challenge. Here are some of the things to look out for because these will really ignite an ADHD brain:

Never humiliate your child. I mean NEVER. Not in fun and definitely not seriously. Humiliation is taken very badly by an ADHD child and they can see humiliation where you might not. I will give you an example. The father of one of my clients wanted to put a video of him as a baby on social media. Despite my 13-year old client begging and pleading for him not to do it, the video went on YouTube. Suffice to say my client's right foot then went through the television screen, and it was only then that the parents realised how humiliated he had felt.

Be very careful how you talk to your angry teen. Anything that can be perceived as humiliation, mickey taking, or putdowns are going to get an immediate angry reaction.

The good news is for most ADHD kids, by the time they hit their very late teens or early 20s a lot of this rage has subsided. They will have mimicked from neurotypical friends how to behave in public and will have learnt how to manage their anger. For a small minority, however, it carries on being a problem in adulthood and an even smaller minority end up in prison because of it.

DON'T EVEN THINK ABOUT . . . doing or saying anything that is going to unnecessarily wind up your ADHD child. Remember they can't regulate their emotions, have a heightened sense of justice and their brain feeds off the adrenaline of fighting.

WHAT WORKS BETTER . . . be careful how you talk to them, don't engage if they are wildly flinging argumentative phrases at you and make your other children aware of the consequences if they purposely annoy their sibling/s. Walk away if you can and it is safe.

What worked and what didn't?

WHEN SIBLING RIVALRY GETS OUT OF HAND

Most ADHD kids will have a variety of brothers, sisters, stepbrothers, stepsisters, half-brothers, half-sisters; some are twins. Their siblings can be older, younger or the same age. Some may live with them and some may be part-time if shared between families.

I've worked with hundreds of families with ADHD kids aged 5 to 18 and I've seen every combination of family situation and the problems that can arise.

First, let's think about the family where there is an ADHD child and other child/ren who are neurotypical. Your ADHD child is going to need special handling. This book will have told you that. So where does that leave your child without ADHD? It can leave them feeling:

- they don't get enough of your attention - all your time is taken up with the ADHD child

- that they are not special - they don't get days off for trips to the psychiatrist, medication or a 'time out' pass at school

- that concessions are made for the ADHD child and not for them

- that they wouldn't get away with the things the ADHD child gets away with and it is not fair

All of this can lead to resentment, hurt, anger, isolation, feelings of low self-worth and low self-esteem. And this will likely have a knock-on effect on how they feel about their sibling/s - ranging from mild dislike to full-on despising! So, my first message in this section is that it is crucially important how you treat your non-ADHD siblings - for their own self-worth. They can also play a bigger part in keeping family equilibrium than you might realise.

First up, I think it is very important they know their sibling is ADHD. I have worked with families who have kept the diagnosis secret. In my view this is WRONG.

I don't think it is of ANY benefit to the non-ADHD children not knowing their brother or sister has ADHD. From as early as they have understanding, I recommend you explain that they have a brother/sister whose brain works DIFFERENTLY. Not worse than theirs, and not better than theirs. But DIFFERENTLY.

It will be a lot for them to take on board. Think about how much information is in this book and then think about your young non-ADHD child taking it all in. It is an awful lot and they don't need to know everything at once. But I definitely recommend explaining a little bit more about their sibling's ADHD brain every time something happens that is ADHD related. For example, your ADHD child:

- Has a major meltdown
- Is unreasonable/violent to their brother or sister
- Has a serious incident at school
- Gets overly emotional
- Punches, kicks or attacks any family member
- Gets in trouble with the police

Always have this conversation when things have calmed down. Probably the next day if there has been a major issue in the house. And always in confidence. You do not want your ADHD child overhearing. This needs to be a one-to-one conversation with your non-ADHD child or children. They need to be able to ask you questions without hurting the ADHD child.

This is your golden opportunity to make the non-ADHD child feel special, and these are my top six tips:

- Treat them like a mini-adult. Don't sugar-coat or withhold information

- Appropriate to age, explain about your other child's ADHD behaviour

- Let them know which ADHD trait this latest incident will have been linked to

- Never, ever lie. Keep it completely truthful

- Make it clear that you have to handle their sibling differently, but that this in NO WAY means they are any more special

- Ask for their help in getting the best out of the ADHD child. Allow them to feel they are important and have influence in the way things play out in future

Trust me, this can be done. Not only have I worked with families where previously it has all been going horribly wrong, I've also worked with families where it all then goes brilliantly. And it only takes a few tweaks for this to happen.

ANGER. It is going to be very useful for the non-ADHD sibling to know that your ADHD child is more than likely going to have anger problems. And that these are directly related to their ADHD. The non-ADHD child must not take it personally that the ADHD child will lose their temper on a more regular basis. Instead, they need to know that this is the way the ADHD child's brain works and the very best thing they can do is retreat and take cover! They need to know that engaging with the anger is only going to make the ADHD child worse. If they want the anger to stop, the absolute best thing they can do is take cover. Literally get out of the way of the storm and wait for it to pass.

This goes against the natural tendencies of anybody when they are being screamed at unfairly. But reassure NT children that the ADHD child's brain is loving the adrenaline arguing brings and is programmed to never give up, will fight to the bitter end and always, always, wants to win any argument.

The ADHD brain will literally keep going on and on and on until it has WON. So, let your NT child know they are never going to win and the very best thing to do is to get out of the way. This really will reduce the ADHD child's rage quicker than anything.

Your NT child needs to know that WINNING in this situation is removing themselves from it.

If you have two or more ADHD kids then life gets even more challenging. Fairness is key and I mean fairness in everything – from who sits on the nice sofa longest to who gets to pick the film to see at the cinema. Your kids may have different types of ADHD - my own house did. Me with my Combined ADHD from my Dad: then eleven years later my brother with a different dad inheriting his Inattentive ADHD. Luckily, it was this way round. He was 'my baby' when he was born and I was 11. He was silent and easy and I adored him. Had the Inattentive one been the older child with a younger Combined sibling it would have been a different story.

It is never going to be a bed of roses when you've got one or more ADHD children in the house. I think if you get your head around that and just accept that knowledge is power, so knowing as much as you possibly can about the ADHD child and what their needs are, is always going to make for a more harmonious home. It is fairly unusual to have two sorts of ADHD under one roof - but not impossible, as my own case shows. I strongly recommend you learn as much as you can about both conditions and what their needs are.

Because of their emotional dysregulation and Rejection Sensitive Dysphoria, your ADHD child could be having emotional outbursts, particularly at the beginning and end of puberty. Remembering that one of the BIG red flags for them is humiliation, the very last thing your NT child needs to do is take the mickey, to tease, even in a good-natured way. They need to understand that their sibling cannot regulate their emotions and some of the displays are going to be quite extreme and shocking. Silence is always the best answer here.

Most ADHD children don't want to be placated or cuddled. They certainly don't want to be told to calm down; they just need to be left to get all their flooding emotions out. And any verbal reasoning you try is going to be met with a "you just don't understand" and more than likely a stream of expletives that just cause fresh waves of emotion.

HEIGHTENED SENSE OF JUSTICE. This is one trait I strongly recommend you educate all your kids on. They are going to get very used to the frequent wail of "it is not fair" from the ADHD one so they need to be aware of where this is coming from. Lack of fairness is at the root of a lot of sibling rivalry. But if you know the rules it is not that difficult to handle. Everything has to be split incredibly fairly. And when I say everything, I mean everything. This particularly relates to screen time and use of Xbox. If you've got children who are sharing devices, then get out your stopwatch and make absolutely sure that everything is split fairly between them. The meltdowns that 'unfairness' cause are just not worth it.

This heightened sense of justice and constant look out for unfairness will permeate every area of your life. Well, every area that the ADHD child wants. There will be some things that they are very keen not to share. For example, laying the tea-table or doing the washing up. But they are going to fight to the death to make sure they get their fair share of anything their brain sees as pleasure.

This is again where your structure and boundaries need to be in place. They must be rock solid, immovable and non-negotiable. For example, if your structure is that each child gets an hour each evening on the Xbox, it is no good estimating times. You will need a stopwatch, a timer, or definitely something that can't be argued with, so your ADHD child knows for sure it is getting what is fair.

REWARD SYSTEMS

Assuming you are utilising these for your ADHD child, they need to be in place for every other child in the family as well. Please don't make the mistake of only using a reward system for your ADHD child. This gives all the wrong messages to your other children. They will see the ADHD child as being rewarded for behaviour they are expected do anyway. For example, if your system rewards your ADHD child for keeping their bedroom tidy and your neurotypical child is doing this anyway, resentment will still soon build.

So collaboratively put together a reward system with your neurotypical children. A good idea is to use this reward system for them to meet their chosen goals. So, for example they might want to complete homework projects by certain dates or commit to netball/singing practice for so many hours a week. Their reward system can be more goal focused than behaviour based. But definitely they need one. Even if they think they don't, I guarantee resentment will build if they see their siblings being rewarded so encourage your other kids to identify goals they want to meet and then reward them. Always make sure these rewards are fair or you'll soon have your ADHD child beating on your door moaning that their rewards aren't as good AND ITS NOT FAIR!!

DON'T EVEN THINK ABOUT . . . assuming your family dynamics will be the same as families where ADHD isn't present. Don't presume your ADHD and non-ADHD kids need the same kind of parenting. If you get the parenting bit right, you won't have the sibling rivalry, or not so much of it anyway.

WHAT WORKS BETTER . . . educate everybody on what is going on in their ADHD sibling's brain. Open and honest communication about why they exhibit ADHD behaviour is crucial. And make sure reward systems are in place and fair for all siblings. And get yourself the best stopwatch on the market!

What worked and what didn't?

WHEN THEY WON'T SHARE

This is a lesser-known trait and doesn't apply to all ADHD children. But the ones it does, it is usually quite severe and can cause problems especially when young.

I've done a lot of research on this and I'm not absolutely sure where it comes from. But my guess is it is possibly the ADHD child liking to keep everything under control. We do like to be 'in charge' and 'to have things our own way' so sharing can be torturous. Also, perfectionism can sometimes go hand-in-hand with ADHD. I certainly have it myself. In this context it means that unless 'everything is perfect' (and that means having everything to myself and everything under my control) I'd rather not do it or have it at all.

It could also come from the trait of our heightened sense of justice. As soon as we start to share something, we can start to feel that the other person has an unfair advantage. And we never, ever, like that.

I remember from childhood that if I was told to share anything, I would rather not have it at all! And this has stayed with me to this day. It doesn't come from petulance - it comes from genuinely wanting something all to myself or I would rather not have it at all.

Anxiety may play a part. I remember a sense of dread that, if I was sharing, I wouldn't get a fair deal.

I see many families with siblings where sharing becomes a problem. The ADHD child wants to do things their way, at their speed and the way their particular brain wiring thinks is better. This can clash with the neurotypical child and also another ADHD child who might see things even more differently! Xbox and PlayStation type games can become a living nightmare if siblings are supposed to share. It is far better to split the time up and let each child have a certain time doing the activity than to get them to share it.

DON'T EVEN THINK ABOUT . . . forcing your child to share if you can see it really makes them uncomfortable or angry.

WHAT WORKS BETTER . . . splitting up the use of Xbox, PlayStation, swing ball, television and anything else into allotted time periods for each child. Give each child control for a certain length of time. If you can afford it, get them one of each of everything!

What worked and what didn't?

WHEN THEY WON'T COME OFF THE X-BOX, PLAYSTATION, iPAD OR ANY OTHER TOY/GAME/GADGET/DEVICE

This may also have been the first chapter you turned to! Before I tell you how to best deal with this, let me explain again what's going on in your kid's brain. Your child's ADHD brain is constantly seeking stimulation. It is never happy 'doing nothing'. It craves stimulation, excitement and for something to be 'happening' – for activity of some sort. Any of these devices mentioned above (and gazillions more) provide a constant array of flickering images, changing pictures, vibrant colours and just about everything your child's brain would kill for. So, first off you need to understand what these devices are giving your child. If you're to have any hope of getting them off them - you need first to understand why they are on them.

Normal life can be quite boring for an ADHD child. What is 'enough' for a neurotypical child is soon going to bore your ADHD child rigid. They just aren't going to be able to 'sit nicely' for three hours and read a book. Or sit and concentrate on a film for two hours. It pretty much definitely isn't going to happen. Unless they're bed-ridden poorly. They need more. They need activity, drama, different things to look at and LOTS of stimulation.

The fact is, when smart phones were introduced, and tablets came on the market all hope of your ADHD child being satisfied with reading a book totally evaporated.

Modern technology, in all its shapes and sizes, really does provide the ADHD brain with just what it is looking for. Nothing needs to stay the same! If they are bored with one thing they can, with the flick of a finger, immediately move on to something new. And as everything is bright, shiny and vibrant this can very easily become addictive to your child's brain.

Because when their brain gets a taste for something that feeds its adrenaline, the brain isn't going to give it up lightly. In fact, it is going to fight you to the death for its right to stay stimulated.

So, this is what's going on when your 11-year-old has been on his PlayStation for five hours. You may well be climbing the walls knowing that this isn't good for him and he MUST need to move and DO something else. His brain, however, is having a party; and the very last thing his brain wants to do, is to leave that party. His brain is compulsively pushing him to stay partying and you are very much the party pooper.

So now you know what's going on, let me tell you the best ways of dealing with this. If you're reading this before it has become a problem, that's good. If this is already an issue it is going to be more difficult to break habits and patterns of behaviour - but we will come to that in a minute. Let's assume for now your child has never been near a device and you are ultra-prepared to put a structure/routine in place, set boundaries and introduce reward systems; because it is a combination of these three that will work best.

Let's start with structure or routine. Nice and simple this one. Your child needs to know how their day is structured and WHEN is the time for devices. Every parent will have their own idea of what is appropriate - but let's say, for the sake of argument, you agree they can go on the iPad for an hour in the morning before school and for an hour in the evening. If your child KNOWS that in the morning their hour just isn't happening until they are washed, dressed, breakfasted and ready for school - and there is NO leeway on that - this is exactly the sort of structure that will work. And almost definitely one structure/routine for the weekdays and one for weekends. Once you've decided this, you need to stick to it. If there's one thing that ADHD kids can't stand and for which they will make mincemeat out of you it is not sticking to what you've said. An ADHD child will kick against structure and boundaries but it is absolutely what they need to function best. So, it is up to you to structure the day in such a way that it works for you and your child and then you HAVE to stick to it. Do not be lily-livered! Do not be fickle! Don't forget your child will see through this in seconds and, trust me, you'll regret it.

Your child, however old they are, needs to be very aware of how the day is structured and this probably means you're going to need to have it written up on a black/whiteboard somewhere. ADHD kids are time blind and have poor short-term memories, so they won't be remembering exactly what times of the day they are supposed to be doing things. There are numerous ways of making this happen but it is definitely a good idea to have a written schedule for weekdays and weekends, kept where it can be seen by everybody.

Next comes boundaries. Remember, your ADHD child is going to push these because that's what their brain does. Again, you have to have very rigid boundaries. It is no good saying to your child "you've got 20 minutes and then your time is up on there" and then forgetting to do anything about it for 45 minutes. Or telling them one day that it doesn't matter if they don't have their breakfast before going on the iPad as long as they have it before school. No, no, no! This is the road to ruin. Do not take it.

You need to make it very clear so that your child understands the boundaries. These are going to be different for everybody, but whatever yours are make it abundantly clear that these are the boundaries and that they are immovable and non-negotiable.

Within these boundaries it is good to give your child options. Your ADHD child likes to feel in charge – but always remember you are ultimately in charge without it being obvious. For example, you might want to give them the option of having the iPad for one solid hour after dinner or having half-an-hour after dinner and half-an-hour after their evening snack. Give the child some options so they FEEL like they're in charge, but always make sure these options fall within YOUR boundaries. If you don't want them on the iPad after 9 pm at night, make sure the options are always for before 9 pm.

And now we bring in the parents of those kids who are already majorly addicted to their devices. You too need to bring in structure and boundaries, but you are going to have a tougher job of it. The way to do this is to negotiate with your child. Speak to them about how much screen-time they feel is healthy and have an open debate about what is right for all of you. Not just for them. For the whole family. Make it a non-judgmental family discussion where all opinions are equally valid. Try and get your child to agree with what is sensible, what gives them time to do other things, what gives them enough time to wind down before bed. Seek their opinion on these things treating them like a mini-adult. You'll be surprised how reasonable an ADHD child can be when they are treated like an adult and consulted for their opinion. Telling them what to do always brings out the worst. Instead consult them and ask for their opinion. You might be pleasantly surprised.

You can also agree to try things out. If your teenager thinks it is very reasonable to stay up till 2 am on the PlayStation and insists they won't be tired for school the next day, agree to trial it for a week. Make a point of asking them at 8 o'clock in the morning how they are feeling? They will inattentively not notice they are shattered, and they certainly aren't going to admit it to you. Saying something along the lines of "I hope you're not feeling too tired and have a really good day at school" (rather than "you look wiped out, you shouldn't have stayed up so late, you idiot") will allow them to realise that it isn't such a bright idea after all - without feeling humiliated.

Your child is always going to need a REASON to come off their device. They are never going to get bored with it, want to do something else or feel it is the sensible thing to do. The easiest way to explain this is that if you are taking away one thing that stimulates the brain, you need to replace it with something else that does the same or similar. You need to give your child something exciting to move onto. 'Exciting' will be different for each child - it could be their favourite TV comedy, chocolate, milk and cookies in bed or anything that your child would look forward to. That, and only that, is going to get them off their device without a fight.

This is also where reward systems come into play. There's lots more information in the chapter on reward systems but you can use these repeatedly to entice a child off a device. Just one example could be that if they come off the device at 8:30pm every evening without any argument every weekday, on a Saturday night they get to choose the family DVD and takeaway. If they fail to do this one night, they lose the choice of DVD and if they fail to do it two nights, they lose the takeaway choice as well. Your child NEEDS something like this to entice them. Something has got to make it worth coming off that device.

DON'T EVEN THINK ABOUT . . . expecting them to come off their devices without there being a reason or because they know they've had enough. Their brain is not going to let this happen.

WHAT WORKS BETTER . . . understand that the stimulation they are getting from the device needs to be replaced in some way. Think about structure and boundaries - Are they good enough? Are they clear? Do you stick to them? Do they need to change? Put them in place by collaborative discussion with your child. And introduce those reward systems.

What worked and what didn't?

WHEN THEIR BEDROOM IS A PIGSTY AND THEIR DISORGANISATION IS DRIVING YOU NUTS

Disorganisation and ADHD go hand-in-hand. What you need always to remember is - we have a disorganised brain! So, having disorganised schoolbags, bedrooms, wardrobes and drawers is the natural progression of that.

However, I can help.

Firstly, you might be one of the lucky ones whose child has at least a sprinkling (or as in my case, a large dollop) of perfectionism which means they will have to have everything very neat and ordered. But this brings with it its own problems because these kids will have a right strop if anything of theirs is not the right way round, facing the front and in its place. I remember being livid once a week, on the day the cleaner had been. She always moved my personal stuff and it incensed me. The first thing I absolutely had to do when home from school was move my Wade Whimsey ornaments back to where they should be in their rightful position. (thanks Jess G for the memory prod there).

But the ratio of ADHD kids with perfectionism is small, so you are much more likely to be dealing with disorganised chaos in their bedroom - and if they have their own bathroom or playroom, almost definitely in there as well.

Before we set about making the best of this, do spare a thought for their ADHD brains. Sometimes kids really want to be organised and they look at their neat & tidy friends in awe at the ease at which they maintain their orderliness. I used to. Much as I wanted my satchel and pencil case to be immaculate, and at secondary my huge school bag, it just didn't happen. No matter how many times I emptied it and put everything back in neatly, it always ended up in chaos. This really perplexes ADHD children because they try harder than others to be tidy, but fail more. We just don't seem to have that neat and tidy gene.

You are never going to change your offspring into that effortlessly structured child, but there are lots of things you can do to help.

Something important for you to know before we make plans is that they say with ADHD 'if we can't see it - it doesn't exist'. So, if you see your child walking round in the same pair of socks, the same T-shirt and the same shorts for weeks on end this is because they were on the top! We will literally only grab what we can see because we don't have any memory of what else we own. Take this info seriously. Even at my grand old age of 50-something, I still wear the same three or four tops and three or four pairs of jeans on a regular basis. I have no time for the other 90% of my wardrobe which I will only have a good root through if I'm going out for a special event. Because we do everything so quickly and because we have no memory, we literally are going to wear the things that are visible. I'm constantly surprised by what I own when I have a good clear out. I have no memory of buying at least half of it and it has never been worn.

So, if you want your children's clothes to get an equal wearing, the first thing you need to do is rotate what clothes are appearing on the top of the pile, in the top drawer or at the front of the wardrobe. It is very doubtful they will notice. They will still grab the first thing they see.

Next, don't give them too much choice. Our brain becomes overwhelmed easily and loads of choice is too much to handle. It is far better to give us an option of red, blue or green shorts than 20 different options. Keeping your children's clothes, toys and anything else in the bedroom as streamlined as you can is your first way of helping them keep on top of things. Think quality over quantity.

Next to think about is storage. I have one word for you. Baskets! Remember what I said about anything out of sight is out of mind? This is why cupboards and wardrobes aren't the best idea. Consider a hanging rail where your child can see all their clothes at once. You can get ones with the pulldown cover so you don't have to look at their clothes all the time, but they are usually much more accessible than wardrobes. Ikea is your friend here.

And baskets work brilliantly. Firstly, you can put labels on them so your child can see from the outside what is inside each one because they sure as hell aren't going to remember. Secondly, you want something that they can walk into the bedroom and chuck things in with the greatest of ease. Even a lid could be the barrier to your child being able to sling something in quickly enough before they're off to do something else. So, invest in some good quality open baskets that you can label with 'socks' 'pants' 'T-shirts' 'school shirts' 'PE kit' and the rest.

Some ADHD kids are prone to hoarding. There are lots of reasons for this and your way round it is to play on their compassionate side: on a regular basis ask them to donate things to charity. Or to give to children younger than themselves who might not have as many toys or clothes.

If your child has a coexisting ASD diagnosis, getting rid of 'stuff' is going to be a lot harder but most ADHD kids will have that compassionate ADHD trait and be willing to give up their own clothes / toys / games to make other kids happy.

Another idea is to set up a garage sale. ADHD children love making money and if you set them up with a car-boot sale table or a garage sale telling them they can keep a percentage of the money and choose a charity to donate the rest to, this will usually motivate them to have a really good clear out.

DON'T EVEN THINK ABOUT . . . shouting at them for living in a pigsty, moaning at them for always wearing the same clothes or leaving them to sort their own storage out.

WHAT WORKS BETTER . . . is taking a good inventory of what's going on in their bedroom. Do they have too many clothes or toys? If so, decide whether it is a charity shop visit, donating to friends or a garage sale that needs to happen next. Talk to your child about what areas they most struggle to keep tidy and go with them to buy storage. If they like their shelf units/baskets, there is a lot more chance of them using them.

Or if you can afford it, get a builder to instal shelving, storage, or whatever you and your child decide will work best. It is not as expensive as you may think, and you really can then tailor it to your child's designs. If they're into fairies and unicorns, fairy and unicorn shelving units are likely to get much more used!

What worked and what didn't?

WHEN FOOD BECOMES A PROBLEM

There could be a lot going on when your child starts having problems around eating and these range from the mildly irritating to the majorly worrying. So, tread with caution before you start yelling at them to finish everything on their plate and telling them that there are starving children in Africa who would love to be able to eat Brussels sprouts.

Some of us with ADHD have more of a compulsive eating problem. When I was a child practically nothing filled me up. I remember my mother angrily telling at me at the end of dinner "Well go and have a slice of bread then!" whenever I whinged I wasn't full. She was thinking a slice of bread was the LAST thing I would want. She thought I was after more pudding. This saw me swiftly exiting into the kitchen and relishing eating bread and butter because I really was still hungry.

So, the first thing to look out for is compulsive eating. Your ADHD child's brain is always telling it that 'nothing is enough'. It needs more. When they eat a meal they aren't listening to their tummy and realising that it has had enough - let alone waiting the 20 minutes recommended to see if it is actually full. Not a hope. Instead, your child's brain is saying "this is nice, this is yummy, I want more". There are a couple of ways of dealing with this. One is having a healthy tin, box or drawer that is full of little healthy snacks your child can have whenever they feel they are hungry. I'm talking about things like oat bars, rice cakes, fruit, small packs of raisins - you know the sort of thing - or carrot sticks and hummus in the fridge. It doesn't go down well when you deny an ADHD kid food, but making sure it is the 'right kind' of food is relatively easy. Make sure there's lots of variety and it is all healthy and don't give them any restriction on it. If you restrict - all you will get is a child like me who was forever sticking her hand in the biscuit barrel grabbing what she could and foraging for food in the kitchen. Far better your child has access to healthy snacks whenever they feel the need.

If your child is at the other end of the scale and gets 'funny' around food there could be all sorts going on. Some ADHD children are very fussy about how their food is presented. I've met ADHD kids who won't have baked beans on the plate because they 'leak' into other food. I've met ADHD kids who will only eat peas if they're in a separate bowl. I've met ADHD kids who won't eat anything with gravy because they like to pick their food up with their hands. And I've met an awful lot of ADHD kids who can't stand sauce of any kind - even tomato ketchup!

And I've met kids like me who are very funny about the texture of things. I can't eat nuts because they taste like cardboard or raisins, sultanas or currants because they are all wrinkly and I can't stand the texture.

Remember too that a lot of ADHD people have Sensory Processing Disorder, me included, so there could be issues around the senses with food. Your child may not even know what's going on themselves so some gentle exploration with them will go down very well when it comes to finding out what they will and won't eat. They might not even know why they don't eat certain things. I certainly didn't realise it was the texture of things I had a problem with until I was much, much, older. For other ADHD children it can be the smell of things, the look of things, the colour of things and whether or not they are crunchy or smooth. There is literally no end to the issues your child might have around food that you might not have even thought of. And if your child has the coexisting condition of ASD, it opens a whole new door to even more problems on a much grander scale.

Another major problem can be sitting at the table to eat when you have ADHD hyperactivity and restlessness. It is not just your child being difficult if they can't sit still. It is this strong and chronic desire to move and DO something that means they can't 'just sit still'. If this really is a problem for them then you have lots of options but do take it seriously into account. You might decide that your child can leave the table whenever they wish as long as they come back to finish their food at the table. Or you might want to let your child sit in the lounge with their dinner on a tray if it means they can relax more with the distraction of television in the background. Come up with options that suit you both. Don't allow your dinner to be ruined by forcing a child to sit at the table when they really can't. Take their ADHD into consideration and make alternative plans. This isn't 'giving in' to them not sitting at the table. It is taking their condition into account and making reasonable and acceptable adjustments that work for you both.

Something else that might be going on is overwhelm. Big dinners can really overwhelm an ADHD person. I remember Sunday roasts being plonked in front of me and feeling a kind of overwhelm and exhaustion just looking at it. And I was a compulsive eater! So, for kids who aren't really interested in food this is just going to be a mountain too big to climb. What works much better for ADHD children when it comes to food is variety. I strongly recommend you consider having tapas-style dinners - several items in bowls in the middle of the table from which your child can dip in and out as they wish. Your ADHD child likes variety and this is going to appeal much more than one big plateful. You can make it as healthy as you like but try not to give them a massive plate with just three items on it. Bowls in the middle of the table with half a dozen items is going to go down much better, especially for finickity eaters.

We also need to take into account eating disorders. I have met both girl and boy ADHD teenagers who have developed binge eating, anorexia and bulimia. It is not hard to see why some ADHD children go down this road. If you consider that low self-esteem and anxiety are usually part of the ADHD condition, it is quite easy to see why eating can become disordered. Keep a watchful eye on your child's eating patterns, particularly as they hit puberty. This is when the ADHD overthinking, low self-esteem, anxiety, compulsive and impulsive brain activity can impact on their eating.

ADHD medication can also severely affect appetite. A lot of children (and adults) report pretty much losing their appetite while their medication is working. This means your child may have very little appetite, if any, during the day but will want to eat like a horse in the evening. Rather than trying to force your child to eat three similar sized breakfast/lunch/dinners in a day, far better is to let them have a small amount of protein in the morning and another small amount of protein at lunchtime. Not only will this help the medication work better, it is also healthy. Then focus on them getting most of their other nutrients in their tea/dinner in the evening. If your child really struggles with appetite, then protein bars and protein shakes can be a good replacement for breakfast and lunch, as long as they are getting a very well-balanced healthy dinner.

DON'T EVEN THINK ABOUT . . . expecting your ADHD child to sit at the table and eat their dinner with no issues at all. Ever. It is unlikely to happen.

WHAT WORKS BETTER . . . be mindful that you might need to be creative and innovative to entice your child to eat. be watchful of binge eating, compulsive eating or restricted eating behaviour. Be prepared to adjust what and how your child eats to suit their particular ADHD idiosyncrasies.

What worked and what didn't?

WHEN THEY START GETTING FUSSY
ABOUT CLOTHES

One of the coexisting conditions of ADHD, and actually one of the most common, is Sensory Processing Disorder (SPD) and this is usually why clothes may become something of an issue in your household!

Most, not all ADHD people have a problem with what materials touch their body. The vast majority of ADHD kids and adults I know won't tolerate anything scratchy, itchy, fussy around the neck or clothing that clings to their body. Nearly everybody with ADHD wants to wear denim, cotton, jersey and loose-fitting clothes. And an extraordinarily large number of ADHD people don't like wearing shoes. Most report that they would spend their lives barefoot if they could. I'm sitting here barefoot writing this!

I'm a classic example of SPD and I remember reacting very violently as a child to my mother trying to put me in a mohair jumper and a scratchy yellow poncho. And polo-necks clinging to my throat made me feel like I was choking. To this day I will only wear denim, cotton and jersey and cut every label, hanging strap and 'spare button' out of clothes before they even make it out of the shopping bag and into my wardrobe.

The chances are that your child too will have issues with clothing. SPD is something you might want to look into as a lot of ADHD kids have it and it can affect ADHD children in a ton of different ways. Some not only have issues with touch but also smell and taste. Certain smells do make ADHD kids feel sick and they might not be exaggerating. Like, I wasn't exaggerating when I told my mother the smell of cucumber sandwich spread made me feel sick. Ten minutes later when she was clearing up the evidence of that, she got it!

Clothing labels are usually a massive no-no for ADHD kids. They irritate the skin and at least 90% of ADHD people cut out their labels before they put their clothes on. So, if your child insists on this, just go along with it. And you might need to consider where you sew their school name-tags into their uniforms, so it won't touch and irritate their skin.

SPD will most likely be the overriding problem your children have with clothes, but there will be other factors that you need to take into account. One is 'fitting in' at school. Your child will probably already be conscious of being different and standing out because of their ADHD, so the one thing they won't want to do is stand out because of their clothes/shoes. If they tell you they want to wear certain things because 'everybody else is' and they will feel more comfortable, let them.

Another ADHD trait that can play a part here is perfectionism - wanting everything to be exactly right. Some even quite young children will get very bolshy about clothes or shoes not being right. I vividly recall my three-year old niece wailing: 'I'm not comfy, I'm not comfy' because I hadn't lined the seam of her tights on her tiny feet as she wanted. Some will be overly particular about there being no stains or marks on their clothes or shoes. Particularly trainers. White trainers with teens will become your own personal nightmare - if there is so much as a tiny stain, you will likely find yourself being asked for new ones.

Something else to bear in mind is that an ADHD kid's body can often be hotter than those of other children. For starters, because they move around so much and are restless and constantly on the go, they can get much hotter and sweatier than neurotypical friends. Also, if they're on medication this can raise the body temperature slightly, so if your child really doesn't want to wear their blazer in March because they are too hot, don't insist that they do. It is not going to kill them and it isn't worth the risk of setting off World War Three!

A quick mention of self-esteem here. It is accepted that ADHD children have lower self-esteem than neurotypical children, so if your child insists something makes them look fat or uncool or is too babyish for them - it really will be easier to just swap the item for something else rather than risk them doing what I did. For two whole years of my school life, I hated the shoes my mother put me in so much that I used to change into plimsolls at the beginning of the day (behind the bike-shed so nobody saw me) and wear them all day and every day. The hated shoes were old-fashioned and guaranteed to have led to name-calling and bullying, which I was terrified of. It was easier to put on my plimsolls and carry my shoes around with me all day. Granted the 'cool kids' at my school were wearing four-inch platform shoes and my mother was right in that she didn't want me breaking an ankle, but it was hell for me standing out as 'different' in a tough school environment.

DON'T EVEN THINK ABOUT ... making assumptions your child is just being fussy, or difficult, or making a big deal about nothing. SPD is a very real condition and gives a lot of distress to people if not recognised.

WHAT WORKS BETTER . . . talk to your child about what material they prefer and what shoes they find comfortable. If they hate something - find out why. Without judging. Try and work with your child so that you find a compromise that suits you both rather than battling with them.

What worked and what didn't?

WHEN THE LYING STARTS

The youngest ADHD child I have actually witnessed lying was four-years old. You might have your own horror story of lies starting younger than this but four is still incredibly early. Much more likely your child will start to slip in the odd lie by the age of around six or seven. This will pretty much always be them getting themselves out of a hole. Or lying about having done something boring like having brushed their teeth when they haven't been within a country-mile of the bathroom.

Lying comes quite naturally to most ADHD kids and I know it is a major problem in some families. So, let's first tackle why ADHD kids may lie and then we'll go into what you can do about it.

Life can be very boring when you are an ADHD child. I remember lying to liven things up and make things a bit more interesting. I also lied to get what I wanted. Particularly in the food department. I became very adept at putting my hand in the biscuit barrel - under the beady eye of my mother - and in one swoop pulling out four biscuits instead of one.

My lies were all little and harmless (apart from my guilt over that poor librarian) but I've worked with hundreds of ADHD young offenders who lie through their teeth. So much so I think they even believe their own lies.

So, if we accept that if your ADHD kid is lying, they are probably doing so for one of these reasons ~

- Boredom
- Wanting to shock or push boundaries
- Wanting to be the centre of attention
- Wanting to get away with not doing something boring like tidying their room
- For personal gain such as 'I've not had any cake so I'm going to have a big piece now'
- Needing to liven things up or make a story more dramatic
- Because they've genuinely forgotten and think they are telling the truth

And, of course, it could be a combination of any or all of these. The first thing you need to do is accept it's quite normal behaviour for a young ADHD person to lie. That's not saying you have to accept it, and yes you have got to do something about it, but don't think it is anything out of the ordinary, because it really isn't.

I also suggest you don't turn it into a game of cat-and-mouse and try to catch your ADHD kid lying. All that is going to do is feed the adrenaline in their brain and make them even more determined to get one over on you.

So, how do you tackle it then? My answer is to make it very clear to them how important the truth is in life. Always remembering that they won't be thinking of the consequences of lying. Give them examples of how people lying in history has caused problems. Find really dramatic examples. Famous people who have been sent to prison for anything that involved lying. There are a good few famous ones to choose from!

:eds to know that lying is never right and however bad : is always better than a lie. Something that works very : them a certain amount of time to admit the truth. If something is a blatant lie, it is very unlikely your child is going to admit it immediately. Remember, they won't want to be humiliated causing Rejection Sensitive Dysphoria (RSD) to kick in. But if you have a '24-hour rule' whereby they can come to you with the truth and there won't be ANY repercussions, you will find a lot of ADHD kids will come to their senses when the heat of the moment has passed. It is a very good idea to allow them to communicate this to you in any of several ways. You need to put some good systems in place whereby your child has a route out of their lie. Sometimes we feel that we can get backed to into a corner and we have to lie to get ourselves out of it. If you make it very clear to your child that that is NEVER the right route - honesty and the truth is ALWAYS the best way - you make it easy and accessible for them to do that. That means giving them lots of choices as to how they admit the truth.

For starters they aren't going to want to do it in front of brothers and sisters because that will be humiliating. So, you need to find a confidential way they can do it. This might mean a text to your phone, a note under your bedroom door or a confidential chat. I strongly suggest you decide this collaboratively with your child. If they have been involved in choosing the ways they can communicate the truth to you, they are far more likely to use them.

And when your child does tell you the truth you need to make a very big fuss about it. Praise them, thank them, enforce how important the truth is and how they made the right decision. The more you do this the more likely they are to admit the truth the next time.

This really is one of the ADHD traits that I firmly recommend you nip in the bud as soon as possible. I've seen far too many ADHD boys in young offender institutes who are adept liars. I'd go so far as to say pretty much everybody is in prison because they lie. There aren't many honest criminals kicking about.

I've also worked with ADHD teenagers of around 17 and 18 who have been getting into hideous problems with the law because of lies. Lies really do need to be stopped in their tracks as early as you possibly can.

There's no need to panic and think this is anything unusual but also don't ignore it. Don't humiliate your child or dish out punishments without trying to get to the bottom of the problem.

DON'T EVEN THINK ABOUT . . . accepting lying, covering up for them or hoping they'll grow out of it.

WHAT WORKS BETTER . . . use the phrase 'not telling the truth' as it sounds a lot less harsh than 'lying'. Speak to them confidentially when you know or suspect they've not been truthful. Collaboratively come up with ways they can tell the truth and come clean after the event. Make it very clear that they won't be punished if they tell you the truth within a certain period of time. Praise and thank them for their honesty.

What worked and what didn't?

WHEN THEY START STEALING FROM YOU AND OTHERS

Not all ADHD kids pinch things but a lot of them do. I don't consider myself a criminal, but I was quite a prolific thief in my early teens. Not only was I swiping sweets from the sweet shop, I was also on a very regular basis filching money out of my mother's purse. This was always for food. And nearly always when we went swimming with the school, and I wanted to get my fair share of snacks from the vending machine afterwards. I remember thinking I was a real clever clogs because I only took coins that wouldn't be noticed. So, for example if she had three 50p's I would only take one of them. This was when I was round about 12 years old.

I cannot recall ever being caught, but that could be my dreadful memory! Anyway I know it went on for quite a long time and I considered myself very clever for not getting caught.

The reason why ADHD kids steal things is, I believe, primarily because of two traits.

1) Our impatience and wanting things NOW. We steal because we don't want to wait, to save up money and then buy something in three months. If we want it, we want it NOW. So stealing is the obvious answer.

2) I think we do it also for the adrenaline rush. There is an incredible buzz to be gained from stealing things - I had it in my early teens. Thankfully, I also had the fear of God put into me by the police who visited the school to tell us the impact of a criminal record on our life. I've never nicked anything since!

As with all things ADHD, you might find this a minor problem with your kid or a major one. I've actually worked with families who have had to put locks on fridges, kitchen cupboards and even bedrooms. One teenager was so notorious for swiping anything, the family had to keep their handbags locked in their bedrooms to be sure he wouldn't be dipping into them.

Some ADHD kids have a major problem with stealing. They literally can't walk past anything that appeals without grabbing it. This can get you into big problems in shops. They will see something on the shelf and have it in their pushchair from the age of three! Honestly. From as young as that. But usually stealing doesn't become a problem until about the age of eight and, as with me, it is highly likely to ramp up as puberty hits.

Once you've realised your child is stealing, it is time for THE VERY SERIOUS TALK. Rather than screaming and shouting, sit them down when you are all calm, and the messages you need to get over are:

- You're not judging them for stealing and you understand that this is probably part of their ADHD. But together you do have to do something about it
- Ask them to explain to you what it is they get from stealing. Are they doing it purely for the excitement or is it because they want things they can't afford?
- This is something you need to tackle together because you don't want this impacting the rest of their life. You are ON THEIR SIDE
- Explain to them how easy it is to get a criminal record
- Explain the likelihood of them needing a bigger buzz, leading onto more serious stealing and more serious problems for them

- Do your research beforehand as to which countries they won't be able to travel to if they have any sort of criminal record. A dodgy past can seriously impact future travel plans
- Talk to them about how they will be limiting their career choices.
- And if they're still not getting the message, tell them how carrying on with such behaviour is only ever going to end up in one place. And that place is prison

If it is money they want, and often it is, talk to them about different ways of earning money. Perhaps you can utilise their skills around the house or garden. Or get them washing cars for neighbours. If they are at the right age, think about a part-time job. Get them earning money early because ADHD kids are usually driven, they want things, but you need to show them how working for it is the much safer and more satisfying route.

Many of the young offenders I've worked with in prison have started stealing in their early teens because they wanted the latest trainers, tracksuits and devices. Not one of these boys had a part-time job. I, however, started working at the age of 12 and had my own money from then on. So, if you can instil a work ethic into your early teen you've much more chance of them not pilfering.

And don't forget the ADHD inability to think of the consequence. This is the serious bit. You can almost guarantee they won't have thought of the consequence of popping something off the shelf and into their pocket. Without chastising them, you need to get the message into their brain that one quick action could have serious repercussions for the rest of their life.

DON'T EVEN THINK ABOUT . . . panicking and assuming this means your child is destined for a life of crime. Don't report them to the police to frighten them. It is very usual for ADHD youngsters to steal and all that matters is how you handle it.

WHAT WORKS BETTER . . . try to be understanding. Communicate openly and non-judgmentally about what they are doing and the consequences. Make sure they know this is an element of their ADHD. Come up with options for them to make their own money.

What worked and what didn't?

WHEN HYGIENE GOES OUT THE WINDOW

For those of you who haven't experienced this yet. I can almost guarantee at some point your ADHD child is going to get very bored with ablutions and not bother with basic hygiene!!

There is one very simple reason for this. Getting showered or bathed, hair washed and dressed is incredibly boring. And mind-numbingly repetitive! ADHD people really don't like doing anything over and over again and especially if they can't see the point. So, having regular showers or baths and washing their hair, and even cleaning teeth, can be seen as really unnecessary and dull.

I am the most fanatical clean freak there is now but during my teens I went through a classic ADHD stage of deciding cleaning my teeth was unnecessary. The next time I went to the dentist I had to have four fillings which hurt like hell and from that moment on I've brushed my teeth twice a day. But it was several weeks, if not months, when a toothbrush didn't go near my mouth!

Equally, bathing was terribly boring for me. So, I went through a patch when I was about 13 of running a bath, sitting on a stool next to it reading a book and swishing my fingers in the water to make my mother think I was in the bath. I don't think this went on for very long before comments were made that I was a bit on the whiffy side, and I must've decided to start washing again.

But even to this day I find the daily shower and hair wash the most monotonous and boring thing I do. I've always said if I could pay somebody to do it for me, I would. And I've met more than one adult ADHD client in therapy who has admitted they can go for days without showering because they find it desperately dull.

So expect your teen to go through a patch of either not showering, bathing, washing hair or cleaning teeth. It really is to be expected and my advice would be to put up with it as long as you can without making a scene - at the same time pointing out how nice certain aftershaves or body sprays are! How nice people's teeth look on the television and any other gentle, subtle hint you can come up with to make them realise their chosen way of avoiding cleanliness isn't great for the long term.

The key really is to make it more exciting or giving them a reward afterwards. Exciting could mean a waterproof radio in the shower or a waterproof television near the bath. Or make it so they don't get their tea or bedtime snack before they have showered. The reward system really does work well here.

Another good way is to buy them gifts of flash designer aftershave or perfumes - footballer ones for boys and popstar ones for girls. You know the sort of thing. Encourage them to emulate their idols. Be that body sprays or aftershaves or shampoo.

DON'T EVEN THINK ABOUT . . . feeling your stinky teenager is anything unusual. Don't criticise them or humiliate them or nag them.

WHAT WORKS BETTER . . . talk to them about ways of making washing more exciting. What would work for them? Would they like a radio, television or something else in the bathroom to liven things up a bit. Make them understand that you know it is boring and it doesn't stimulate their brain. So, look for ways together to make this activity more fun.

What worked and what didn't?

WHEN THEY WON'T OR CAN'T GO TO SLEEP

Sleep is a big problem with ADHD. In fact, it is only very recently they've decided that having a sleep disorder isn't a comorbidity of ADHD - it is part of the condition. You are likely to hit problems with sleep early on. Parents report babies who 'never slept' or 'took hours to settle' or 'needed constant stimulation'. These babies grow into Hyperactive or Combined ADHD toddlers. On the opposite end of the scale – generally Inattentive babies are sleepy-heads who will sleep for ever. And they get very grouchy when they're woken up.

First off - going to bed and sleep is BORING for so many ADHD kids who will fight the whole routine. They won't want their night-time shower/bath, to brush their teeth or get into bed because their brains are saying "This isn't exciting. Let's stay up longer and have FUN". Yep, really! My brain still does this today. No matter how shattered I am, sometimes my brain just won't calm down and shut up.

So, if your child starts kicking off about going to bed, remember it is because it is their brain wanting them to stay awake. Not just them being contrary!

There are ways of dealing with this and the best is to make bedtime more interesting. I hesitate to use the word 'fun' because what you are needing to do is calm their brain down. BUT there are ways to stimulate your child's brain enough to get it to want to go to bed without a fight.

So, let's deal with getting your child actually IN to bed before we deal with getting them to sleep, which is a whole other ball game.

To get your child faintly interested in the bedtime process, I strongly recommend you put a reward system in place.

These need to be highly individualised because what will float one ADHD kid's bedtime brain won't float another.

But reward systems generally work VERY well at bedtime. Because, quite honestly, going to bed and shutting down our brain is pretty much the toughest thing we have to do each day. And the torture is worse because it is EVERY DAY. Day in, day out! I know many ADHD adults who still hate the bedtime routine and find going to sleep the hardest thing they do every day.

Let's assume you've got your little angel in bed with whatever reward system worked (one always will - it can just be trial and error finding it) you've now got the issue of getting them to sleep.

First of all, don't make the mistake of thinking it is easy! The "just shut your eyes and go to sleep" routine will not work with most ADHD brains. I remember being told this numerous times as a child and it made no sense to me at all. Instead, there are tons of things you can do to help your child sleep. In no particular order they are as follows:

Melatonin is recommended for ADHD children who struggle to sleep. You should be able to get this from your GP and it is relatively easy to order online as well. You can buy it in a 'Gummy Bear' from Amazon even. Melatonin helps most ADHD children sleep and a lot of parents swear by it.

Weighted blankets. I've no idea actually why, but almost certainly because of our sensory issues, a lot of ADHD people like to have pressure on top of them and feel 'safe and protected' and therefore more able to relax and go to sleep. Be careful because there are a lot of cowboys out there charging small fortunes for weighted blankets. There is no need to pay those crazy prices. Instead look for a local seamstress who can make you one or do a very thorough internet search before committing.

Anything that will calm down an ADHD brain is always going to be helpful. Aromatherapy can be good. Burning some particularly relaxing oils in the room like lavender and chamomile can definitely help. Also sleep hypnotherapy works. Ideally, this needs to be played on a constant loop at a low volume - just high enough to be heard but not loud enough to be annoying. There are also some very relaxing projector visuals like moons and stars that you can play on the child's ceiling. Amazon is a good source for these.

Reading is a great way to calm down your child's brain before bedtime. A book or comics, ideally not Kindle. And always get your child off any screens a minimum of an hour before trying to get to sleep, ideally longer. Do make sure any tablets or phones they are using switch to 'blue light' rather than 'bright light' from early evening onwards.

There are no magic answers when it comes to sleep. Insomnia really is part and parcel of having ADHD. And it is much more of a problem for some than others. For me it is always been the worst part of having the condition.

ADHD medication can also make matters worse. You have to be very careful if your child is starting on stimulant medication and it majorly impacts their sleep. Keep in regular touch with their psychiatrist/meds prescriber because poor sleep over a long period can be seriously detrimental to health. It can impact their mood, behaviour and performance at school. Lack of sleep can also be dangerous because it makes kids far less attentive and distractible when doing things like crossing the road. Sleep is imperative for mental and physical health, but can be very, very difficult to achieve. It is really a question of trial and error, and trial again.

Something to be aware of is Delayed Sleep Phase Syndrome (DSPS). This is a condition not solely applicable to ADHD, but a lot of ADHD people have it. I do. It is where your circadian rhythm is approximately four hours out of sync with 'normal'. So, instead of getting sleepy around 10-11pm a DSPS brain will keep going until around 4am and prefer to sleep until lunchtime.

Not all, but most Inattentive ADHD kids have no problem sleeping. My Inattentive brother would amaze us sleeping whole weekends in his teens. Their problem is usually that they feel sleepy and tired too much.

But most ADHD kids have problems getting their brains to shut off, so I suggest trying everything you possibly can! My bedroom at night has aromatherapy, hypnotherapy AND prescribed sleep medication ALL battling to get my brain to sleep.

DON'T EVEN THINK ABOUT . . . it being easy for ADHD kids to 'just go to sleep'. It is not easy! Don't compare them to non-ADHD siblings. Different brains mean different sleep patterns.

WHAT WORKS BETTER . . . Asking your GP for melatonin. Making bedtime reward focused - give them a reason for wanting to get into bed. Hypnotherapy on their mobile. Aromatherapy burning through the night. Mobiles or pretty lights on the ceiling.

What worked and what didn't?

WHEN THEY START GETTING INTO TROUBLE WITH TEACHERS

It is going to happen. Even the best behaved 'got it under control' ADHD kids are going to hit problems at school for two simple reasons. WE DO NOT LIKE AUTHORITY and WE HATE BEING TOLD WHAT TO DO. These are consistent ADHD traits that apply to the Inattentives, Hyperactives and Combineds. So it is a pretty much given that schooling is going to become a problem.

If you're lucky it won't be until puberty hits from about age nine or ten onwards. ADHD is a hormone connected condition so when those puberty hormones start jangling around their body, prepare to take cover. But a lot of ADHD kids don't run into major problems at school until their early teens. I didn't. Infant and junior school were pretty much a breeze. Secondary school a different story.

But for others, from around the age of three upwards, their 'not being able to sit still', 'needing to move about', 'distraction' and 'inattention' will bring problems from day one. Even at nursery school for some.

For these characterful cherubs you need to start having regular communication with their teachers/nursery staff. Don't assume the teacher will know more about ADHD than you. Odds are they won't. As I write in 2020, ADHD barely features in teacher training. I know, it is shocking! At best, their teacher may be aware that ADHD is 'something to do with impulsivity, hyperactivity and distraction'. And that really is at best. I can guarantee they won't have been trained in the dozens of traits you'll be well versed in now you've read this book. So, to get the best help from your child's teacher you may well have to train THEM.

ADHD is a condition covered and protected by The Equality Act 2010. This means you are permitted to ask for 'reasonable adjustments' at school that take into account your child's disabilities.

Each ADHD child will present differently. And have different needs. For example. Some ADHD kids need extra time in exams as they struggle to concentrate/focus on what's required and get distracted. Others need to be able to leave the exam early because they do everything at breakneck speed and will cause disturbance and disruption if they have to sit twiddling their fingers.

'Reasonable adjustments' you might want to request include a 5 or 10-minute time out card. This gives your fidgety/angry child the time to nip outside for a run around or to let off steam. Most schools will authorise this once a diagnosis is in place. Some even when you're going through the diagnosis process. So it is worth asking.

Fidget toy. These are a bit of a contentious issue. It is true that most ADHD kids need to fiddle/doodle or do something with their hands all the time. It is the constant movement/stimulation that calms their brains down enough to concentrate. I know. Sounds weird. But it is true! If you want to see an agitated ADHD kid - ask them to sit perfectly still for 5 minutes.

I was a doodler at school and filled dozens of notepads with dot to dots, filling in the gaps or drawing random shapes and filling them in with biro pen just to keep me from going bonkers from boredom. I still do it today.

However, it is also true that some fidget toys can be a tad noisy and a lot of schools have banned them for annoying other students.

There are quiet versions, so push this point with the teacher and insist on your child having SOMETHING to keep their fingers busy.

As your child gets older it is ATTITUDE that usually kicks in. Tons of ADHD traits feed into this. It'll almost definitely be a combo (or the full whammy) of having no respect for authority, not liking being told what to do, always thinking we know best, wanting things to be done our way and the biggie - only respecting people who show us respect (not high on most teachers' list of priorities!) So, from 11-ish upwards things can go from being 'a bit rocky' to 'off the scale nightmare' for ADHD kids at school.

In my own case I simply thought most of the teachers were thick. Such was my arrogance! I used to point out their spelling mistakes on the blackboard with obvious glee. I was right, they were wrong.

But I was 'mildly' badly behaved at school thanks to a strong-willed mother, who I was terrified of, sitting at home always ready to give me a rollicking. Depending on the severity of your child's ADHD, coupled with the level of understanding/respect each teacher gives them, means you could be in for some corker behaviour. Be prepared.

It is not unusual for ADHD kids at school to throw things, kick things, shout out, talk too much, get distracted and struggle to concentrate. Their ADHD traits will be raging as the hormones do their best to unsettle them. In nine out of ten cases, this is because they are bored OR think they are being treated unfairly. FAIRNESS is very important to ADHD kids. This is because we have that HEIGHTENED SENSE OF JUSTICE. So, if something doesn't seem fair to us, watch out. You're going to get a reaction. And unlike a neurotypical brain, ours just won't let it go. Never in the history of a furious ADHD kid did the thought "just let it go" come into their outraged head.

So how can you help your ADHD teen have a smoother journey through education? It is the C word. No not that one. COMMUNICATION! TALK to their teacher(s) – always remembering they probably know next to nothing about ADHD. Explain the idiosyncrasies of your own child's ADHD brain. Be clear what your child needs. As ADHD presents quite differently, we can't expect teachers to know exactly what each ADHD child needs. Better still write up some notes. Give a trait, then bullet point underneath how this presents and how best to handle it. Like this -

Distraction -

- He will look out of the window or be in his own head

- Ideally say his name to refocus him. Shouting or humiliation will bring on anger

One of the biggest problems is how teachers talk to ADHD kids. Shouting, humiliating, or talking to an ADHD child in a degrading way is a massive NO-NO. But trying to get teachers to alter the way they speak to kids isn't easy. If they are of the mind that shouting is the only way to get children to do anything, you are going to have the devil's own job getting them to talk to your child differently. The key really is getting the teacher to understand that talking to an ADHD child in an aggressive or demeaning way is never going to get the best response.

I've been into several schools myself, training teachers, and almost without exception they do take on board that how you talk to an ADHD child is going to affect the behaviour and performance you get out of them. But there is always, ALWAYS one teacher who looks at me steely eyed as if to say, "over my dead body" and that is always the one that the child is going to come up against! Guaranteed.

Here's a very good example as to why this is SO important and it is worth hammering this point home with all their teachers:

I adored my English teacher. She treated me with respect, allowed me to read the part of Macbeth in class for two years solid for my

O level - all the other parts changed weekly, but I suspect she'd sussed I was best kept occupied. So I enjoyed the classes, worked hard and achieved an 'A' grade in English.

My maths teacher, however, was rude, dismissive, passively aggressive and in my eyes very disrespectful. I'd come first out of 132 pupils in English AND maths on entering the school, but I loathed this woman so much that when it came to the O-level I wrote my name, the date and then sat back and wrote absolutely nothing else. For three hours, all the time thinking: 'F**k you, take that you old witch'.

There's not many who leave school with an 'A' in English and 'U' Ungraded in maths. But I did. And now I know I'm not alone. WILDLY DIFFERING GRADES is an indicator of ADHD. Because we will give our all in the subjects we love. And our brains just won't get stimulated or involved in subjects we don't. Or when we've clashed with a teacher.

Dialogue with teachers is crucial. Choose your wording carefully. You're not asking teacher(s) to grovel at your child's feet and accept disruptive behaviour. But you can explain to them that -

- shouting
- humiliating
- sarcasm
- singling out

Is pretty much guaranteed to bring out the worst in an ADHD child.

What works tons better is an understanding of ADHD and 'questioning' rather than 'telling'. I know many parents who have run reams of ADHD info off the internet, put it in files and handed all the relevant bits to teachers. It is worth the effort.

Then to be mindful how they interact. To ask questions instead of telling. For example: "How would it be if you tried doing that this way" instead of "You've done that wrong. Do it this way". The different ways those two different phrases are received by an ADHD brain are huge.

Questions work VERY well with ADHD. It makes us feel that we are in charge. Like our opinion matters. Like it is our choice.

Another issue impacting in class can be the ADHD trait of DIFFICULTY UNDERSTANDING INSTRUCTIONS AND DIRECTIONS. This is a big one in school. Our brains sometimes just don't know what the teacher means. I remember very well the cold chill of fear that went down my back when we were instructed to pick up our pens and write when I didn't have a clue what I was supposed to be doing. A quick glance over my neighbour's shoulder usually sorted that out. Once I'd seen what the teacher MEANT I could crack on and usually finish before anybody else. But struggling with instructions and directions is a much lesser-known ADHD trait and one you might have to explain to teachers.

Boredom in class is always going to be a problem for ADHD kids. Make sure the teachers are aware of this. If not, your child is going to be angry and disruptive for no apparent reason. They are more likely going out of their minds with boredom. The answer? Keeping busy and occupied. 'Being the clown of the class' is a massive indicator of ADHD. ADHD psychiatrists will always ask if this was you. It is born of boredom and not being stimulated/stretched enough. For example, I was an angel in English but a prize buffoon, always clowning around in maths. Ideas to run past your child (before suggesting any ideas to the teacher). Would it help make classes easier if -

- they were moving about and allowed to help the teacher by collecting finished work, distributing handouts and other odd jobs

- running errands for the teacher

- allowed books to read when finished work early

- allowed to do homework in class

Another ADHD trait possibly impacting at school is SOCIAL ANXIETY. Look out for this, especially in boys. It is one of the biggest comorbidities of ADHD. It could mean your child will be unexplainably uncomfortable (or downright bolshy) in groups, and this includes classrooms. They won't know it is social anxiety. And they'll probably cover up the anxiety by being aggressive and rude, even violent. If they're not keen on shopping malls, concert venues, busy public transport and such like, dig a bit deeper. There could be more going on.

DON'T EVEN THINK ABOUT . . . assuming your kid's teachers automatically know about your child's ADHD and individual needs. Don't assume they have had any training in ADHD. Don't chastise your child for bad behaviour at school till you've dug deeper to find out what the problem is.

WHAT WORKS BETTER . . . ADHD kids can't help getting bored. Or distracted. Don't tell them off for it. Instead work with their teachers to find different ways of doing things that work for your child and don't disturb the rest of the class.

What worked and what didn't?

WHEN HOMEWORK BECOMES A NIGHTMARE

There are two types of ADHD kids when it comes to homework. There is me and the rest! Or that's how it would appear. I was radically different to most ADHD children in that I wanted to get my homework done and out of the way the minute I walked in from school. It can't just be me. There must be other ADHD kids like this.

I remember rushing through the front door after school and heading straight to my bedroom and cracking straight on with all the homework I had been set. For me I couldn't enjoy my play time until the work had been DONE.

I did it all in double-quick ADHD time and was chapters ahead of my peers in all the subjects, according to my mother.

If you have one of THOSE kids, you don't have too many problems. I was like this right through from age 5 to 17. It never changed and even at college years later, I still did my homework and 'got rid of it' as soon as I possibly could. I think this is possibly due to that perfectionism trait and the dreaded sense of overwhelm. If I could keep on top of things by doing them quickly, I had much less chance of being overwhelmed and feeling out of control. Being in control has always been very important to me.

However, it is highly likely your own kid doesn't have this attitude towards homework and that would be far more common!

For most, homework is pure torture. And an irritating and intrusive continuation of what they've been hating all day. To have schoolwork 'leak' into their home life and encroach on their own time is a major frustration for a lot of kids.

And this particularly relates to ADHD boys. ADHD girls, generally speaking, fall into the "I'll comply even if it annoys me, and it'll be last minute - probably at midnight or on the bus into school" category. Boys often, not always, but definitely often, fall into the "I'll find every excuse under the sun not to do it. And if you force me, watch me kick, scream, shout and generally make your life hell for BULLYING me into doing something I REALLY DO NOT WANT TO DO".

It is this last challenging lot we will deal with here!

Firstly - please remember. Your child could well be dealing with an undiagnosed coexisting condition of ADHD that is making studying way harder than it should be. I was. It took till I was 56 to work out I had, and get a diagnosis for, dyscalculia. Never heard of it? Neither had I at school. But it is more commonly known as 'the numbers version of dyslexia'. And it is the reason I failed my 12+ exam. One of the traits of dyscalculia is 'not being able to solve problems'. So that was my grammar school education up the spout. It was also the reason I received a 'U' for maths and 'A' for English at O-Level (thanks Bucks Education for not bothering to notice that this was clearly indicative of a learning disability). Bear this in mind if your child is bright and having absolutely no issues with English and history, but flounders dismally with maths, economics and any subjects involving numbers.

Also look out for signs of dyslexia. Especially in girls. It is very common. Also, dysgraphia which makes putting words down on paper difficult.

Don't assume that the psychiatrist who assessed your child necessarily picked up all these co-existing conditions. I've met countless children (and adults) where the diagnosis of ADHD has been given but the comorbidities haven't even been investigated. And it is important. Really important. The Rejection Sensitive Dysphoria (RSD) part of your child's brain is not going to want to be humiliated for being slow or getting bad marks. So, they'll cover up. Usually by mucking about or kicking off. Case in point - maths was where I was at my most witty and entertaining. Where my 'clown of the class' ADHD trait was most prominent. I couldn't get to grips with what was being taught so entertained/stimulated my brain myself this way instead. So, look at the subjects with which your kid is struggling. Which subjects do they 'hate', which homework do they want to tackle least, and then dig deeper to find out what's really going on.

Once you're sure there are no learning disabilities affecting your child's ability to do homework, we can assume it is any one of the myriad of ADHD traits that are coming into play.

Take your pick!

- procrastination
- lack of motivation
- not being excited by it
- boredom
- not liking to be told what to do
- not seeing the point
- having no respect for the teacher, or what they require of them

Any or all of these could be coming into it. It doesn't really matter which ones are impacting your child, all that matters is what you do about it. And these are my top tips.

Firstly, put your child in charge. Let them decide when and where they are going to do their homework. This needs to be a conversation you have when things are calm and there is no friction in the air. It may well be that your child needs a quiet place or a noisy place or a place on their own or a place where they can see you. Each child is different. Find out what they need and where they need it.

Until you know different, believe your child. If they tell you they need music on in the background, let them. If they tell you they need their headphones on, let them. If like me, they need absolute silence and the door shut and their annoying younger brother kept well away, make sure it happens. If it turns out they were having you on and listening to loud music really isn't conducive to them working well, you will need to gently and with encouragement point this out. Don't do it accusingly. Remember you are always on their side and want the best for them. Encourage them to try alternative environments or stimulation levels. It really is one rule for one and one for another. I've met teenagers who flunked GCSEs because they were put in a room with no posters on the wall, so they had nothing to look at to calm themselves down. I've known others fail exams because there was too much noise and too much activity.

Most children work best when their homework is broken down into chunks. If they know they've got to do 30 minutes work followed by a cup of tea and a biscuit, they are going to work much better for those 30 minutes than they would have done for 45. You will need to structure this with your child and put alarms either on their phone or an egg timer or something they can see. Usually, an ADHD child can work flat out for a short period of time as long as it is followed by a break.

When children are little, to keep ADHD children from being distracted and inattentive when they are young, it is usually best to sit with them while they do the homework. It will be better for you to spend 30 minutes making sure it gets done rather than nagging them for two hours and it doesn't get done. As they get older, they will want to be more in control, and this is fine - but they are still going to need help with structuring their homework times.

As always, reward systems come into play here. If it costs you the price of a DVD and a takeaway on Saturday night, it is worth that to have your child do their homework each evening with no nagging. I've seen parents use everything from 50p a day to a football match ticket for Tottenham as incentives. Whatever it takes it will be worth it – both for your sanity and their education. Something nice to look forward to after homework is a necessity!

Also worthy of note - tutors usually work extremely well for ADHD children. Kids like the one-to-one attention, it means they can learn at their pace if they are particularly fast or particularly slow, and it is much less easy to get distracted when you are the only one in the class. I've known many ADHD teens to be struggling hugely at school and then flourish within weeks of studying with the right tutor. It is well worth looking for a tutor who is experienced in ADHD and any other coexisting conditions your child might have. Especially if it is something like autism. You really want a specialist and they do exist.

DON'T EVEN THINK ABOUT . . . expecting your child to just sit down and do their homework without any fuss on a regular basis. Don't shout at them and expect them to be able to do their homework like any of their neurotypical brothers and sisters.

WHAT WORKS BETTER . . . sit with them and do their homework with them until they are old enough to do it on their own. Then make sure you decide collaboratively where its best they do their homework, what environment is going to work best for them, whether they need white noise or complete peace and quiet or music or headphones.

Then decide collaboratively the sort of length of time they feel they can study for without needing a break. Make sure those breaks have something nice enough in them for your child to aim for - whether that's a hot chocolate or a cuddle with the dog.

Finally, think about having a reward system that rewards them at the end of the week and the end of the month for such things as doing their homework on the right day, without nagging, and handing it in on time.

What worked and what didn't?

WHEN THEY CAN'T OR WON'T REVISE

Now this is something I think might surprise you. ADHD brains HATE revision! And there's a clue in the word - it is the 'RE' bit. It means repeat or re-do something. That is never going to stimulate an ADHD brain. So, getting your children to revise is going to be one of the biggest nightmares you'll ever have! However, what I'm going to tell you now works - so listen up!

I could never understand why I couldn't revise. I wanted to revise, I wanted to do well in the exams, and I knew that revision was the key to it. But boy, was it a massive struggle. I couldn't concentrate on the paper - if I'd read something before it just did not stimulate my brain enough to read it again and my short-term memory was so shocking that nothing stayed in anyway.

So go easy on your kids around revision time. They will be surrounded by friends talking avidly about how much revision they've done, and your ADHD kid will probably have a ton of anxiety because they know they haven't done the same amount. And it won't necessarily be because they're not bothered. They might be very bothered but just not able to do it. So here are a few tips.

ADHD brains learn best at the last minute. I actually got up at 6 am on the morning of my English Literature O-level to finish reading *Cider with Rosie*. Cramming at the last minute meant I passed with a C because my brain took the information in 'in a crisis', when the adrenaline was flowing because I hadn't been able to finish reading it before. ADHD brains work best in a crisis when the adrenaline is flowing. Therefore, your child is going to learn and store the information much better as the exams get closer. So there really is no point putting a six-month revision plan in place - there are other things you can do that will help.

ADHD brains need to be stimulated and that means by something new. There are lots of alternative ways of getting information into your child's brain, but the least effective will be them sitting down looking at text. So, you need to get your thinking-cap on and come up with different ideas. These are ones that I've seen work in the past - but you will no doubt come up with your own. Let's take English as an example. If your child is studying a play, take them to see a live performance of it where possible. Outdoor performances where you can take a picnic are always a good bet because they can fidget/move without being told off and nibble food and drink to keep their hands occupied.

Go to the cinema to see a big screen version of the play. Buy them the audiobook, if available, or the DVD. If they're studying Shakespeare, and it is within your means, visit Stratford-upon-Avon and the William Shakespeare Museum. Try and stimulate their brains around the subject. ANYTHING is going to be better than just reading the boring text.

Think about the subjects they are studying. There is a huge number of museums/places to visit that might be relevant to other areas of their learning.

Because their brains are likely to accept information as they get closer, put a structure in place that means they have plenty of time for study in that last couple of weeks before the exam. That really is when most of the information will sink in. Don't go organising social events, take them on holiday or plan lots of play dates around this time. It really will be in that last 2 to 4 weeks that their adrenaline will kick in and much more of the information they are learning will stick.

Rewards work when trying to get children to revise. They learn best in short bursts with a reward at the end. So, when the adrenaline is flowing and they are in learning mode, make sure you structure it, so they get regular breaks and a reward at the end. Even if that reward is fish and chips or a takeaway of their choice, with their reward-based brain they are much more likely to commit and learn if they know there is something good coming at the end of it.

Another good tried and tested tip is to write facts on Post-it notes and have them visible for your child, whether that's in their bedroom, on the fridge, in the dining room or where they study. Helping them write up facts, dates, and information they need to learn on Post-it notes and then moving these around with them really works. Because they are brightly coloured and in small segments they are much more likely to remember it. So, if they're studying in the kitchen, lounge, bedroom or dining room they can take the relevant Post-it note with them.

Another tip that really works is testing your child. If you remember that ADHD brains like to win and rise to a challenge, getting them to do some revision and then you testing them on it is a brilliant way for it to stick in their brain. You can make this fun and you can add in rewards to stimulate your child's brain even further. I used to love being 'tested'.

All ADHD kids are different when it comes to the best environment to revise. I could only do it in complete silence. However, I know of many children who need white noise or the television on in the background before they can concentrate enough to take in information.

And if motivating your child to revise at all is difficult then remind them that with ADHD in adult life, they won't like being told what to do and they will want to have all the choices. If they don't get the grades they need to get into college or to study whatever they have chosen, all those choices get taken away. Get across to them that as much as you know revision is difficult, it is crucial if they want to have all the best choices later on in life.

DON'T EVEN THINK ABOUT . . . assuming revision is easy if they just put their mind to it and it is just a question of them sitting down and looking at a book for long enough. It really isn't and that won't work.

WHAT WORKS BETTER . . . be creative. Think of different ways of getting information into your child's brain. Think cinema, DVD, theatre, events, museums, YouTube, Googling. Any different way of presenting that same information to your child which is exciting and not boring.

And remember they are going to revise best at the last minute so don't panic six months before exams. Start thinking about it six weeks before!

What worked and what didn't?

WHEN THEY WON'T COME OUT OF THEIR BEDROOM

This is typical teenage behaviour but with ADHD there could be a bit more going on.

ADHD kids can get VERY frustrated, irritated and angry in their teens. This can be with just about anyone and anything but particularly brothers, sisters and parents. They can feel anger about a whole host of things so locking themselves in their bedrooms is sometimes their way of dealing with it. I'm not talking on an occasional day. This underlying angst – "being annoyed about everything" can go on for years.

It certainly did for me. From the age of about 14 I wanted nothing other than to shut my bedroom door and ignore everybody. Even going downstairs for tea was annoying because I had to listen to other people's boring conversations and answer what I believed to be very boring questions about my day. I knew what had happened in my day and had no desire to share it with anybody else. Small talk and general chitchat were of no interest to me whatsoever.

I firmly believe the worst thing you can do is force your child to socialise if they are really not up for it and it puts them in a grump. Because a grump can become verbal and lead to shouting/anger and a whole lot of resulting problems. Far better is to let them have their peace and solitude in their room and reappear when they're about 18 and in a better post-puberty mood!

Don't assume they are doing nothing in their bedrooms. Remember their busy brains have racing thoughts and keep them very occupied even when they look like they are doing absolutely nothing.

Personally, I wouldn't go so far as letting them have their dinner in their room. I've seen this happen and it leads to too much isolation. Far better is to encourage them to come out for their dinner and then to leave them to their own devices.

There are no real rights and wrongs with this one but I definitely wouldn't see it as a problem if your teenager wants to spend an inordinately huge amount of time in their bedroom.

DON'T EVEN THINK ABOUT . . . forcing your teenager to spend time with the family if they really don't want to. Remember there is more going on in their head than a neurotypical teenager and after a busy day at school, they may want nothing more than peace and quiet and their own company.

WHAT WORKS BETTER . . . the times you do see them, make sure you ask them if all is okay and if they need your help in any way. Always ensure that they aren't hiding away for any more worrying reasons. If it really is just because they want to be on their own or their brothers and sisters are annoying the pants off them, leave them to the solitude of their bedroom. Not exchanging pleasantries with Aunt Flo on the sofa or watching Top Gear with Dad really isn't going to do them any long-term damage.

What worked and what didn't?

WHEN THEIR FORGETFULNESS IS DRIVING YOU POTTY

This is a big issue for anybody with ADHD. So, a bit of scientific fact for you first. Short-term memory is a major problem for kids and adults with ADHD. Bizarrely long-term memory is fine so we can often remember things that happened 10 years ago but not 10 minutes ago. This is all to do with the brain wiring.

It is also because, as a reputable ADHD psychiatrist told me, "For a thought to become a memory it has to be thought for so many split seconds and an ADHD brain rarely thinks a thought long enough for it to be stored as a memory".

That's a gem not many people know.

So, first of all, you need to get your head round the fact that an ADHD kid's short-term memory really can be shocking. It can be so bad that some young adults go to the GP convinced they've got early onset dementia because they cannot remember what they did five minutes ago. Your child won't be aware their short-term memory is poor, so sometimes they will outrightly lie and believe it is the truth because they genuinely won't remember. For example, your "did you clean your teeth" question may get a "yes" answer because they've already forgotten that they haven't even been in the bathroom yet that morning.

It is usually when they start school that forgetfulness and short-term memory become a real problem. I could list 100 things that a child can forget in a day. But regulars are forgetting to bring their homework home, forgetting to bring their PE kit into school, forgetting to take the required textbooks in each day, forgetting to bring a school report/letter home, forgetting to take their lunch, forgetting even to eat their lunch, forgetting what homework they've got to do that night. The list goes on!

Before you bought this book, you may well have become exasperated with their seeming lack of care and attention to these things but so much of it can be caused by almost zero short-term memory.

Medication does help with this and so do visual reminders. One thing you need to dispense with is attempting to get them to remember to do things by keeping it in their head. That's a complete and utter waste of time. An ADHD child needs a visual reminder to remember to do things. This is again when Post-it notes come in extremely handy. I have clients who have put Post-it notes in school lockers saying 'Tuesday - don't forget to bring your homework/PE kit/lunchbox home'. This works.

So put reminders on their phone if they're allowed to have it with them in school. And reminders in their bedroom to take things to school. But it needs to be visible. It needs to be bright. And ideally it needs to be movable like a Post-it note so they can carry it with them as they move through the house. - as trust me, a child can forget something when moving from one room to another.

Writing things in a notebook is no use at all because an ADHD child could easily forget to take the notebook or forget in which notebook they wrote things. This is why Post-it notes are so fabulous. They are cheap, colourful, bright and can be moved around with the child. They also give satisfaction and a self-esteem booster shot when you screw them up and throw them away knowing that thing has been achieved.

Short-term memory is worse for some people than others. Mine was fine as a child but worsened as an adult.

DON'T EVEN THINK ABOUT . . . losing your temper or being impatient with a child who forgets to do lots of things. Don't roll your eyes heavenwards when they've forgotten something. They almost definitely can't help it.

WHAT WORKS BETTER . . . talk to your child about what they think might work for them. Make suggestions and try out new memory-jogger systems. Make it a fun learning experience with your child as to what works to prod their memory and make their life easier - and what doesn't. And put Post-it notes on a recurring order from Amazon!

What worked and what didn't?

WHEN THEIR PROCRASTINATION IS DRIVING YOU NUTS

Now this trait is a lot stronger for some with ADHD than others. Personally, I rarely have it unless something is exceptionally boring - like accounts! Mostly people with Hyperactive or Combined ADHD don't procrastinate anywhere near as much as people with Inattentive ADHD. However, we ALL become masters at it when something is extremely boring. But it is those with Inattentive ADHD who seem to be able to procrastinate over just about everything and this can be infuriating if you are a parent.

What you have to remember with your kids is procrastination IS an ADHD trait. They are not just being lazy layabouts to get on your nerves or because they can't be bothered.

What their brain is actually saying to them is "this isn't exciting enough for me to get stimulated about. So, I'm not doing it. At most I might do it later. But the odds aren't good".

Lack of motivation and procrastination are right high up there in the list of how ADHD 'impairs' somebody. Sometimes our procrastination even drives US nuts but there is very little we can do about it. Yet again it is medication that can make the world of difference. A little example for you on that. One morning when I took a stimulant medication I spent 2 1/2 hours sorting out some receipts and accounts that I had been ignoring avidly for the past year. It wasn't until the afternoon that it suddenly clicked why I had managed to do it - the procrastination was eradicated by the medication. So, if you've been putting off medicating your child for any reason and procrastination is a real problem, it might be worth revisiting the possibility of meds. It really can make all the difference.

There are a few tried and tested ways round this, but before we move onto those, I must let you know of another reason why ADHD people sometimes procrastinate. Believe it or not it is perfectionism. Perfectionism can be part of ADHD and it can make a lot of kids and adults procrastinate. Their thinking is that unless they can do something perfectly, they don't want to do it at all. I've met grown ADHD adults who have procrastinated for years because they weren't sure they could do a project properly.

So, what could look like chronic procrastination to you, might actually be somebody wrestling with a project knowing that if they can't do it perfectly 'what's the point' of doing it at all.

The best way to motivate your child to do something if they are procrastinating, is to give them a reason to do it. That reason needs to be in the shape of a reward. I remember as a child only being motivated to do my homework if I did it BEFORE my tea. If I'd have left it till AFTER tea there was just no reason to do it! Nothing to look forward to! I had to have the reward of dinner to look forward to, to get through the homework. Unknowingly, I had worked out how to handle my ADHD from quite a young age. I'm talking 8-9 ish.

This is actually quite a simple trait to handle. Whatever it is you want your child to do, tell them there is something nice at the end of it. It doesn't have to be something costly. For me it was just my dinner every night that made me do my homework. For your child it might be the same. Or they might get access to their iPad when they have finished their homework. A lot of parents of ADHD children I know say that there is no television until homework is done. You need to stick to these rules, but they do work. Nothing motivates an ADHD child like a nice juicy carrot at the end of it.

They will find plenty of other things to procrastinate over, not just their homework. But the same rules apply. They will need a reason to do something and that can be a very simple reward. Their brain needs something to aim for and a reason to do something.

As for perfectionism. You need to encourage your child to do a small amount of whatever it is you are wanting them to conquer. Let's say it is their room that they just don't want to tidy because they don't think they can do it perfectly. Encourage them to start with just the dressing table. Or just one drawer. Allow them to see that they can do small chunks perfectly and then move onto the next section. ADHD overwhelm means that sometimes we can procrastinate because a task becomes overwhelming and we don't think we can do it perfectly. So breaking things down into much smaller chunks really works.

Goalsetting also works with ADHD procrastination. If your child is procrastinating over a lot of things, odds are they are struggling with overwhelm at the same time. Writing things down, either in a diary, journal, notebook or on their phone, can make things look a lot less overwhelming. Get it out of their head so they stop overthinking it. Written down, things always look much less overwhelming to an ADHD person.

And you could help your child schedule getting tasks done and focusing on how they will feel at the end of it. ADHD people do tend to get overwhelmed and despondent when they look at the bigger picture. Encourage your child to look at the small picture. If they complete one tiny chore/task every day, at the end of the week they would've achieved seven things - and at the end of the month thirty. You can motivate your child by explaining if they just spend literally five minutes each day, by the end of the month they will have chalked up thirty achievements. And a cherry on top will be if you give them a reward for achieving seven things and also thirty things.

DON'T EVEN THINK ABOUT . . . screaming and shouting at them that they are lazy, need to just get up and get on with things, are using excuses to not do anything and are hopeless, useless, lazy, worthless and any other negative adjective.

WHAT WORKS BETTER . . . talk to them about what needs doing. Try to understand their thoughts on the issue. Ask them what would motivate them to achieve what needs doing. Make sure they feel in charge of what how they go about things. Help them make a schedule and set goals to achieve tasks. Set them rewards for achieving what needs to be done.

What worked and what didn't?

WHEN YOU JUST CAN'T UNDERSTAND WHY THEY GET SO EASILY DISTRACTED

This is a nice easy one to understand. Their ADHD brain is constantly looking for something more exciting. You can bet your life that if your kid is concentrating on his Xbox, distraction won't be a problem. But sit them down with their homework and it is a different matter, isn't it!

Distraction is a real issue for ADHD kids because their brain is always looking for something different. Something new. Something more exciting. Something to get their juices flowing.

This is a bit of a random example, but I'll tell you how bad distraction can be. I have a strong memory of an English class when I was 14. I spent the whole fifty minutes looking out of the window deciding whether I wanted to be an actress ON stage or do stage-managing BACK stage. I can vividly remember that whole thing in my head, but have absolutely no clue as to what was being taught in the English lesson! One thing I can be sure of though - it certainly wasn't enough to keep my brain occupied.

Distraction is worse for some ADHD kids than others. Some seem to be in a constantly distracted state and really struggle to focus and concentrate. For others it is a minor problem. But it will definitely rear its ugly head when anything boring crops up.

ADHD medication helps with distraction. You should notice the difference if your child goes on it. Suddenly they will be able to focus and concentrate without too much difficulty. Perhaps without ANY difficulty. It really can be quite staggering the difference ADHD medication can make.

There are ways of managing distraction. I don't particularly like any of them. An example could be if your child is doing their homework, for an alarm to go off every 10 minutes reminding them to focus. I think this is a bit harsh and personally it would annoy the life out of me! And environment is key – what will be distracting for some kids, won't be for others.

As your child gets into their teens, getting distracted is likely to affect their education if they aren't on medication.

DON'T EVEN THINK ABOUT . . . accusing your child or telling them off for not concentrating and getting distracted, thinking they have a choice.

WHAT WORKS BETTER . . . understand why their mind wanders. Is there anything you can do about it? Do they need alarms on their phone? If they are on medication and still getting distracted a lot, is it worth speaking to their psychiatrist to see if they are on the right medication, or would another one help more.

What worked and what didn't?

WHEN INATTENTION CAUSES PROBLEMS

The first time I realised how shockingly inattentive I was, I was doing the first of four driving speed awareness courses (yes, I know. Don't judge me. These courses are full of ADHD people). We had to do a 'hazard spotting' test on the computer. I thought I was rocking it. Clicking my little mouse every time I saw something hazardous on the road, I was sure at the end of it I would've spotted more hazards than anybody else. How wrong was I. I'd only spotted about half of them. This was years before I was diagnosed ADHD, so I just chastised myself for not looking hard enough. But it stuck with me. I didn't understand it.

The other time I shocked myself was in Tenerife. On the last day of a girly holiday one of my girlfriends said "I'll meet you at the entrance to the pool. The one with the snooker table".

I didn't have a clue what she was talking about. This was only a small hotel with two entrances to the pool. And there were no snooker tables! Bear in mind this was the last day and I'd spent seven days going in and out of this pool area.

After a five-minute stand-off with me insisting there were no snooker tables in the hotel, she walked me to one of the two entrances and lo and behold there was a big snooker table. I had walked past this thing for seven days and not noticed it. This was also years before my ADHD diagnosis, so again I just put it down to my own stupidity.

Now I realise both these examples are because of my very strong inattentive tendencies. From around the age of five I remember my mother wailing frequently, "watch what you're doing" as something else went flying. I was forever knocking things over, bashing into things, going to pick something up and instead knocking it over. Neither of us knew why I did this, but I did it a LOT.

Now I'm older and wiser and know that inattention plays a very big part with most ADHD people. It simply means we don't notice things. And rectifying this is nowhere near as simple as you just telling your child to pay attention. They can't. Their brain just does not do it. Any of the following behaviour in your child could well be down to their inattention:

- Falling over/tripping up
- Knocking drinks over
- Going to pick something up, missing it so damaging/breaking/dropping it
- Losing things. Because they've not paid attention to where they put it
- Not hearing instructions or directions because they weren't paying attention
- Forgetting what they are doing halfway through whatever it is

The list is endless. And whilst this is perplexing and infuriating for parents, it can also be incredibly frustrating for the ADHD person. I wish I could cure my inattentiveness, but it still features on an annoyingly regular basis.

Don't forget the first two words in ADHD stand for 'attention deficit'. That's how much of a problem inattention can be. Of the numerous traits it gets top billing!

So, if your child tells you they didn't notice something or didn't see something - instead of calling them a barefaced liar, give them the benefit of the doubt. If I can be incredulous about my own inattentiveness, then your child may well do things that stretch your imagination.

DON'T EVEN THINK ABOUT . . . underestimating the impact of inattention on your child. And don't think that by just pointing it out to them, they will suddenly become attentive.

WHAT WORKS BETTER . . . look at different ways of doing things. If they are forever knocking over drinks, buy them a trendy water bottle with a lid. If they are always knocking into a chair, move the chair. If they are always dropping their phone, get them an industrial-sized protective case. And accept that there will be times when their inattentiveness will shock you. Try to work with it rather than criticise it. And never, ever, take the mickey out of them because of it – leave your 'Are you as blind as a bat!' comments unsaid.

What worked and what didn't?

WHEN THINGS HAVE TO BE JUST RIGHT - AND PERFECTIONISM

It is quite common for some people with ADHD to have perfectionism. This might seem like a massive contradiction if your own kid's bedroom is disorganised chaos and they don't seem to give a toss about anything - let alone where it goes! I've no idea what percentage of ADHD people also have perfectionism - or anankastic traits - as it can also be called, but it is quite a chunk and most of these appear to be women. I've got it myself. Fully diagnosed and all.

Perfectionism isn't to be confused with Obsessive-Compulsive Disorder (OCD). Whilst admittedly there is a lot of overlap, full-blown OCD will always have negative thoughts attached, such as. "If my tins aren't all facing the front and up the right way - my dog will get run over." Perfectionism doesn't have the negative thoughts attached. But that's not to minimise the effect of perfectionism. It can have a huge impact on someone. If I explain how it affects me, it might help you understand the magnitude.

For me things have to be exactly 'right' or I can't function. 'Right' can be different things to different people but for me it is all to do with cleanliness and tidiness. A psychiatrist once asked me how I would feel if all my tins in the cupboard weren't facing the front and up the right way. I couldn't answer. He saw the look of abject terror on my face. Eventually I stumbled out, "it just wouldn't ever happen".

As 'disorganisation' is a widely known ADHD trait, how can ADHD then be linked with perfectionism? I've my own theory on this. I worked it out from my own ADHD brain! I believe some of us hate the natural chaos and mess we create, BUT because we aren't naturally neat and tidy, we have to work twice as hard to keep things in order. From this constant battle - and I mean 24:7, year in, year out - comes the mania that leads to perfectionism. Here is one example. I have to be on top of my washing. If the pile of laundry gets too high, I literally can't function. I feel overwhelmed/behind which leads to feeling sad, hopeless, useless and incompetent. It feels like I will never be on top of it all, or my life again. Because I don't want to feel like this, I'm a woman possessed with emptying her laundry basket on a crazy, stupid, regular basis. Bingo, there you have it! Perfectionism! If your child is displaying stubborn behaviour and insisting on things being 'right' look deeper into why. I'll give you some examples of how this might present ....

- Not wanting to go to school because one item of clothing isn't right.
- Not wanting to do homework because the computer/textbook/pen isn't right.
- Not wanting to eat because something isn't right (because a pea touched a fish-finger is one of my favourites!).
- Not wanting to go to certain places/events because the journey/venue/catering/music 'isn't right'.

Remember - perfectionism in ADHD is born from anxiety, so try and be as understanding as your health and temper will allow.

Much as you might want to strangle your 11-year-old who now won't eat his fish-fingers because they have got the wrong fish in them (true story) after having happily eaten them before, understand for him it is now not a possibility. He really is not just being difficult.

Perfectionism is not something anyone would choose. I'd pay good money to get shot of mine. So do a lot of research on the subject if you think your child may have it.

DON'T EVEN THINK ABOUT . . . pushing them if they really are insistent that they can't do something. Don't scream, shout, make threats or punish. This will only increase their anxiety.

WHAT WORKS BETTER . . . ask what the problem is. Help them identify it. They might not even really know. What would make things right? What needs to change for things to be right? It is often something quite minor. Try and understand where they're coming from. Avoid the screaming match. It won't get you anywhere. Communication and understanding will.

What worked and what didn't?

WHEN THEY GET OVERLY EMOTIONAL - EMOTIONAL DYSREGULATION AND REJECTION SENSITIVE DYSPHORIA

This is a biggie. It is now accepted in the medical world that the biggest impact of ADHD on a person is Emotional Dysregulation. Just let that sink in for a minute.

Not hyperactivity. Not inattention. Not impulsivity. Not distraction. Nope! Emotional dysregulation is what affects and impairs us ADHD's MOST.

For the scientists amongst you - Google 'emotional dysregulation and ADHD'. There's lots of info online. But for those wanting the general gist - it means that the bit of our brain that is supposed to regulate emotion doesn't work as it should.

I don't want to sound all doom and gloom, but this can be the cause of serious mental health issues so keep a close eye on the balanced (hopefully) mood of your ADHD kids. Especially teens when the hormone imbalance kicks in too. Look out for this in girls particularly around menstruation time as the combination of emotional dysregulation and raised hormone activity can send your ADHD girl into a whirling dervish of mixed emotions.

Not being able to regulate emotions can mean we become really upset when a TV character gets sick but don't shed a tear when a family member dies. The 'normal' emotional response often just isn't there.

This can lead to some very inappropriate responses as your kid may come over as unkind and uncaring. Actually, more likely they couldn't help wetting themselves laughing when Granny fell over and smashed her face on the pavement.

The opposite can be true. You may find your ADHDer sobbing uncontrollably, desperately upset about something most people would brush off. This is when ADHDers get accused of being overly sensitive or 'always wanting to be the centre of attention' or called a 'drama queen'. Many a time when leaving counselling sessions with young ADHD boys in prisons, I sat in my car and sobbed. Their stories broke my heart.

This is all standard stuff for a dysregulated brain. Add in to this something you may never have heard of and something that is particular to ADHD brains alone. Rejection Sensitive Dysphoria. RSD for short.

There are two elements to RSD.

1. ADHD people do not take rejection well. Particularly humiliation. So, don't ever take the mickey out of your ADHD kid! Don't forget the teenager who put his foot through the television when his stepfather just wanted to put a baby video of him on for the family. That, for him, was humiliating and too much to take.

2. The second element of RSD is ADHD people can perceive rejection when it is not even there. And we are SO good at this. If there's rejection to be felt, we will find it. And it will hurt. Just as much as proper legit rejection.

I can't stress enough how much this trait impacts on the whole life of somebody with ADHD. It can be exhausting having emotions you can't control. Many a time I've been sitting down feeling perfectly happy when a wave of low mood has hit me for absolutely no reason. Only now do I know this is because of the emotional dysregulation. Half an hour later I feel fine and have no idea why I felt dreadful before.

I've had many parents tell me they can't understand how their child can be happy one moment and then miserable the next. They think the child is faking one or other of the moods. I can assure you this isn't the case. We literally can be happy, then sad, then happy, then sad, then happy, then sad all in one day. It is genuine and it is exhausting to live with and there isn't a whole lot you can do about it apart from medication, which does even out emotions, when its working properly.

DON'T EVEN THINK ABOUT . . . telling your child off for acting like a drama queen for 'crying over nothing'. Remember that their emotional response could be different to yours and everybody else's. Try not to accuse them of being overly sensitive or wanting to be the centre of attention because it probably isn't the case.

WHAT WORKS BETTER . . . allow your child to talk about how they are feeling. Listen to them without judging. Very soon their dysregulated brain will move them on from whatever high/low emotion they are feeling, and your best tactic is to not berate them for being moody/weepy but to listen calmly and wait for it to pass. Accept the fact that their emotions will be 'all over the place', especially during puberty and DON'T react to their mood swings. Try and remain constant. A cuddle usually goes a long way – not always, but often.

What worked and what didn't?

WHEN YOU SUSPECT OR KNOW THEY ARE SMOKING WEED

Depending on your view of cannabis/marijuana this could either be a minor irritation for you or a major problem. In my experience the vast majority of teenage boys with ADHD use weed to a lesser or greater degree. I haven't got a clue on the percentages (and even people purporting to can't possibly know the true figure), but from the thousands of ADHD teenagers I've worked with, I would say around 80% of the boys have smoked weed in their teens. A dramatically lower percentage of girls use it, but it is still not uncommon. There are two overriding reasons for this. All of them tell me that it calms their brains and helps them sleep.

However, the last thing I'm doing is advocating the use of weed because I've seen the damage it does. I've seen both the short-term paranoia and the long-term brain damage, so please don't think I'm any sort of advocate for the use of cannabis. And I have never, ever, used it myself.

But I have sat in front of trillions of boys in their teens and 20s who tell me they use vast amounts of it. A lot of them do it every day and those who don't do it as much, usually do it at night because it helps them switch their brain off to sleep.

There's lots of information out there for parents worried about a child smoking weed so I'm not going to regale you with all the facts and figures and whether it leads on to harder drugs. Instead, I am going to tell you how best to deal with your ADHD teenager who is using it.

Firstly, if they are hiding it from you and you have found out, let them know. But don't do it in any sort of judgmental, shouty or angry way. Instead sit down and have a grown-up chat with them about why they are using it, what it does for them, where they are buying it (which is crucial) and always, always check that they are not giving it to their friends or selling it. Giving it to friends means they could be arrested for 'supplying' and selling it obviously makes them a drug dealer. A lot of teenagers don't realise that buying it off someone and then selling it for the same price to their friends means they are any sort of drug dealer! The police view it another way - and I've met many, many ADHD boys in prison for supplying or dealing weed.

The reason you need to know where they are buying it is for their own safety. I could tell you a good few hundred stories of boys who have got into trouble by using dodgy dealers and stories of parents having to get involved in paying dealers off. There is no correct legal way to buy weed, at least not in this country, but you can make sure your child is doing it as safely as possible. If they're doing it in public or by visiting a crack-den where harder drugs are being dealt this is obviously riskier than buying it in somebody's private home.

I strongly recommend you don't panic about this situation but understand it is quite typical for ADHD teens to experiment with weed. Try not to judge and try not to make demands. The more you demand they stop, the harder they are going to dig their heels in. And then they will start doing it behind your back which is much more dangerous.

You are far better off opening up the communication around weed, understanding how they think it is helping them and trying to find alternate ways to do the same thing. So, for example, if they are using it to help them sleep, look at different ways of helping with that without the use of weed.

It is often a sign that your child isn't on the right ADHD medication if they are smoking weed extensively. If they are on the right one, they shouldn't have the need for anything else to calm their brain and if they aren't sleeping there are legal avenues to go down that are far less dangerous than using cannabis.

Do your own research on the damage weed does and communicate this in a positive way with your child. Rather than saying "you're going to end up on heroin and dead in a ditch" which isn't really inspirational, try "I'd hate for you to end up with terrible paranoia, so do try and keep your use as low as you can".

DON'T EVEN THINK ABOUT . . . panicking. Or judging. And don't make demands for them to stop immediately. Don't threaten to report them to the police.

WHAT WORKS BETTER . . . open up the lines of communication. Make sure they are buying and smoking it as safely as possible and encourage them to become educated around the effects of weed. Help them make grown-up decisions on whether they are prepared to risk chronic paranoia, psychosis and potential long-term brain damage. Even the most stubborn of ADHD teens doesn't usually want this and if you are on their side, helping them make the best decision for them, even the most determined weed smoker will see the reality of its long-term use. And don't forget, your local Drug & Alcohol Service will be able to offer free help and advice.

Be honest with their ADHD psychiatrist about the level of use because it will affect the impact of their ADHD medication.

If you see things getting worse, their usage going up and you feel it is getting out of control - find your local addiction charity and go to them for advice. With luck they'll offer counselling for you/your child.

What worked and what didn't?

WHEN THEY START GETTING IN TO TROUBLE WITH THE LAW

This may be the first bit you have turned to in this book and if it is then I've got a lot of information for you here that is hopefully going to help so firstly – DON'T PANIC and DON'T CRY.

It is incredibly common for ADHD kids to get into trouble with the law. So, know that YOU ARE NOT ALONE. Dozens of parents of ADHD kids are entering this nightmare every day of the week - all over the world.

There are numerous reasons for this, but the main ones are these:

ADHD kids get a real thrill/buzz/adrenaline-shot from stealing things.

And that's just for starters. I've mentioned earlier that I used to steal as a 12-13 year old. And I became extremely adept at it! Every Friday my mother would pull up outside the newsagents and I would go in to collect the family comics and magazines, which were a weekly treat. It was a very old newsagents with all the sweets laid out in rows between me and the shop keeper. As he turned his back to get the magazines, I hastily and swiftly filled my pockets with chocolate bars and sweets. I did this for quite a few months.

I can't begin to tell you the absolute buzz I got from doing it. It is still probably the most thrilling thing I have ever done. I wasn't frightened of the shopkeeper catching me - I was confident I could predict his turning round in time to stop. But I was scared my spoils would fall out of the heavily slanted, shallow pockets of my navy-blue school raincoat in the car. I was more terrified of my mother's reaction to my thieving than of any shop keeper!

I can still remember the extreme adrenaline rush this gave me which is perhaps why I understand the tens of thousands of ADHD young offenders in prison for doing pretty much the same thing.

Firstly, understand that whatever your child is up to is probably giving them a massive dose of adrenaline. It might not be stealing although that is the number one reason ADHD kids first get into trouble with the law. Also, up there at the top of the list is 'criminal damage' because they do like to kick - especially when they're having a meltdown. Other highly probables are assault, fighting and drugs. All of these will be giving your child a thrill which their brain will be absolutely loving - and wanting more of.

Next, we need to take into account the ADHD traits of risk taking, thrill seeking and having no respect for authority. You don't need me to explain why those push your kid into doing naughty stuff. The threat of parents, teachers or police pale into insignificance compared to the incredible thrill and excitement.

Boredom comes into play here too. I've lost count of the young offenders I've worked with who say they committed their crimes because they were bored.

Add into these traits the fact that ADHD kids are often restless, wanting to get out and DO something. That 'do something' can easily turn into something risky. Quite simply because anything boring doesn't appeal to the brain.

And another huge factor is that an ADHD brain doesn't have the ability to think of the consequence. They will think of the initial excitement without thinking of the consequence for one second.

Medication should help greatly so if they are not yet on ADHD medication, or (as is common) have stopped taking it at the point of getting into trouble with the law, can I urge you to consider getting your child on medication, pronto. This should reduce the need to be doing something to fulfil the risk-taking and thrill-seeking urges and should also allow your child to think of the consequences of their actions - which they just won't do without ADHD specific medication.

There are two scenarios I'm going to talk you through.

One is where the police are already involved, and the other is where they aren't. Let's start with when they aren't.

If you manage to catch your child doing something illegal and the police are not involved - now is the time to take very swift and positive action. If you have the funds, book them straight in with an ADHD coach, one who understands fully the impact their behaviour is going to have on their life. Either way these tips will help.

The most crucial bit of advice I can give you is that you must let your child know you are ON THEIR SIDE. If you take up an oppositional position, things are definitely going to get worse. And potentially a lot worse. And the more distance you create in your relationship, the more your child is going to enjoy shocking/annoying you with their behaviour.

Whichever parent is communicating best with the child at this time (if you have the choice of two), get them to have a very quiet but serious conversation away from everyone else. It is imperative that you let them know you are ON THEIR SIDE. They need to know that as long as they are being honest with you, you have got their back and will do everything in your power to get them out of the current situation.

Next, they need to appreciate the severity of the situation. Without scaring them and without telling them off, you need to help them understand the impact of what they have done. Remember their brain won't automatically have thought of the consequences so you need to explain what the worst-case scenarios could be, at the same time assuring them of your absolute commitment to helping them get out of this situation. These consequences could be having a criminal record, limited career options and reduced travel opportunities. A top tip - they could have thought about going to prison - but they won't have thought that they might not be able to go to America. Do your fact-finding about their particular criminal activity and what could be the long-term consequence.

When you talk to them about these consequences it is very important you do it from a "thank goodness we've caught this early, and if you change your behaviour now these things won't affect you" angle. Always keep it positive. Everything you say can be presented in a positive light - remember how you speak to an ADHD brain is very indicative of what response you will get.

Once they have understood you are on side, make it very clear that they have to be brutally honest with you about everything they have done in the past so you are fully aware of what you are dealing with. Also make it clear that you understand blips may happen again in the near future and the ONLY THING you ask of them is that they are honest with you. Reiterate how you will not judge; you understand that ADHD drives them to do certain things but if you are to get them out of this situation, they HAVE to be absolutely honest with you, to give you the best chance of helping them.

At this point you need to let them know that blips are part and parcel of life. Nobody is ever going to be 100% perfect and with ADHD they are prone to making more mistakes than other people - especially as they are growing up and entering the adult world. There are going to be lots of opportunities to screw things up. However, the more aware they are of how their brain operates, and the more honest they are with you, the more you can both keep blips to an absolute minimum.

I can't stress the importance of letting them know there will always be blips. My work with offenders in prisons proved this. When I was trying to get the naughtiest of boys to change their behaviour, once they had accepted that a blip didn't mean a failure and also didn't mean they weren't changing their behaviour long term, they were honest with me when one happened and we used each of them as a learning opportunity. I can still remember their little faces as I walked into the room. Before I'd sat down they'd be telling me of their blip – so desperate were they to be honest. I never chastised, always congratulated them for being honest and then we dissected what had happened and put in place how they wanted to handle it next time.

We used every single blip as a learning opportunity. What worked, what didn't. What might have made a difference. Analysing their actions makes them 'pay attention' to what they inattentively did before without thinking of the consequence. Pure ADHD. You can help them see things differently. The very fact that you tell them you know there will be blips, guarantees there will be a lot less of them in my experience.

Remember ADHD brains are reward based at this point. So, a whole list of negatives is not going to help you. What is going to help you is telling your child any of the following that is relevant -

- By being honest and changing behaviours now, they are giving themselves the best chance of keeping all their options open when they get to 16.

- By being honest and owning up to their mistakes now, they can avoid having a criminal record.

- Having no criminal record means they can go in the forces if they choose to. They won't be restricted in any of their career choices.

- Changing their behaviour now means they won't be restricted as to which countries they can travel to, often for the rest of their life.

- Remind them that ADHD people do not like being told what to do. Yet if they carry on with their criminal activities all those choices are going to be taken away. The police and subsequently possibly the prison/probation service will be telling them what to do, when and what to eat, when they can sleep, and controlling every aspect of their day. No ADHD person wants this. Make it abundantly clear to your child that they still have ALL the choices and if they want to be in charge of their own life they need to change their current behaviour.

- Make it very clear to them that this is THEIR choice. If they want to choose a life with no freedom and being told what to do, it is absolutely their choice to carry on their illegal activities. But if they want to be in charge of their own life, they need to work with you to change what they are doing and quick. Remember ADHD people do not like being told what to do, so you have to make it very clear that all the choices are in their hands.

If you take this approach you have the strongest chance of your ADHD child changing their behaviour. This works in about 90% of cases. The other 10% are kids who are hellbent on a criminal lifestyle and with those you've really got your work cut out. For these exceptionally strong-willed, bullish characters you may well need to bring in outside help. There are charities who specifically work with kids like this. My own, ADHD Liberty, has funds available to offer highly specific counselling to keep vulnerable ADHD kids away from a criminal lifestyle. But don't you give up, even with the most difficult teenagers. You need to be consistent, positive, always on their side and gently pushing for them to make the right choices. It is probable that at some point they will realise what you are saying makes sense. Expect them to fight you every step of the way but do not give up! You'll need incredible resilience, and it is always wise to call in help from other members of the family who can communicate most easily with them. Often, this could be an auntie, uncle, or grandparent. I've worked with the most prolific offenders for years who suddenly have that lightbulb moment and realise what I'm saying makes sense. So don't give up. You could be in this for the long haul.

Now for the alternative scenario, when the police are already involved. All of the above still applies but in addition I strongly recommend you find a solicitor who understands ADHD. They do exist, and as time goes by more and more of them are becoming aware of the condition and its link with criminal behaviour.

Since I left the prison service, I've been working in private practice specialising in helping ADHD teens and young adults who are finding themselves on the wrong side of the law. After a lot of research, investigating countless recommendations and actual court proceedings, and by a ruthless process of elimination, I have managed to find some of the best ADHD solicitors and barristers in the country. Get in touch with me and I'll help.

My strong advice to you would be to not entertain engaging a solicitor who doesn't have extensive experience with ADHD. If your child also has a diagnosis of ASD it is even more important that the solicitor has knowledge of both conditions.

It is not a given, but in every court case I've been involved in, as long as the solicitor has a thorough understanding of ADHD, the diagnosis has been enough to keep the ADHD child out of prison. Should your child not yet have been diagnosed, or medicated, or on the right dose of the right medication, these factors also play a huge part in the judge's decision and go in your favour. Keep a list of the important dates, diagnosis, dose of what medication they had and for how long and communication between you and their GP/ADHD psychiatrist. This can become critical in court.

Don't just assume that your local reputable solicitor is going to know enough about neuro diversity to represent your child. I've seen parents go this route and it has always gone horribly wrong. Just having 'a good solicitor' isn't good enough when you are dealing with ADHD. They need to know about all the different ADHD traits, how they have impacted on your child and their connection to crime generally and the particular crime specifically. Ideally enlist the help of an ADHD coach to instruct your legal team on the different ADHD traits that will have exacerbated the crime.

It can be a hugely scary time for families when ADHD teenagers get into trouble with the law. Often, the families themselves are very law-abiding, highly-respected professional people and are horrified that a member of the family has become involved with the police. Try to stay calm. Know that this is very probably happening right now to another family in the next town to you, if not the next street. It is very, very common and with the right legal support and with your child knowing you are completely on their side, there is a way through.

I know many families who have been distraught when the police have entered their teenage child's life but with the right help and the right attitude from you, you really can navigate through this. Colleges and universities all over the UK are full of ADHD kids who nearly screwed it up completely - but turned it round. Look at some of the best ADHD examples out there – Sir Richard Branson went to prison at 20 for tax evasion. It is totally possible to change your child's life path.

DON'T EVEN THINK ABOUT . . . going into a massive panic. This has happened before, and it will happen again with ADHD children. Don't feel like your world has ended and this only happens to you. Don't feel alone and don't feel you have to get through this on your own. There is help at hand. And don't take the oppositional stance with your child. Don't argue, scream, shout, be irate, cry, chastise and make them feel worse than they possibly already do, even if they are playing the big 'I am' to your face.

WHAT WORKS BETTER . . . keep the lines of communication open. Let your child know you are on their side. Assure them that you will get through this together. Seek help and always deal with legal professionals who fully understand ADHD.

What worked and what didn't?

WHEN THE QUESTION OF MEDICATION COMES UP

Before starting this section I'm going to make it extremely clear that I am in no way medically qualified. I am not a GP, psychiatrist or psychologist. I am but a humble counsellor who works with hundreds of ADHD clients. What I'm about to tell you has been gleaned from my experience with parents giving their children medication, and children/adolescents taking it. It is their experiences that I will be using, hopefully to give you a better understanding of what ADHD medication can do for your child.

Usually when your child is first diagnosed you will be given the 'option' of medication. Psychiatrists typically leave the decision of whether to medicate or not up to you and the vast majority of parents find this scary and unhelpful. They've no idea what they are supposed to do and there is hardly any information out there. So, I will try hard to fill that gap for you. Please always remember this is mine and my clients' experience and is NOT medical advice. For that you absolutely must speak to an ADHD psychiatrist.

The initial reaction of most parents to being offered ADHD medication for their child is "not on your life". The thought of putting medication into their precious poppet's perfect tiny body is the last thing they want to do. And I understand this perfectly. I really do.

ADHD medication is notoriously confusing but trying to keep it simple, there are two main types. Non-stimulant and stimulant. Stimulants nearly always work much better for ADHD but for people who can't tolerate the stimulants then the non-stimulants are an alternative. Stimulant names that you will hear banded about are Elvanse, Concerta and Dexamphetamine. Non-stimulants are Strattera and Guanfacine.

Knowing what I know now, I think NOT trying medication is nearly always the wrong decision. And I don't say that lightly.

You see by not giving your child ADHD medication what you are in fact doing is forcing their brain to work 24/7 in the way it doesn't want to. Your child will be having to force their brain to focus, to concentrate, to sit still, not fiddle, not get bored, not be distracted, not say and do things impulsively without thinking of the consequence, not joke, not be the clown of the class - because that's what it WANTS to do and you are going to be asking them to NOT do that without any assistance whatsoever!

You also aren't giving your child the best chance at their education, because the medication helps them concentrate and focus. Crucially, medication also helps them retain information. Remember 'An ADHD brain rarely thinks a thought long enough for it to be stored as a memory'. How difficult is it going to make revision for your child if they don't have the benefit of medication helping them retain their thoughts?

And this isn't just going to affect them at school. Think about them going on to college and perhaps even university. Asking their brain to override itself through all those years is going to be taxing and they will pay the price. I don't want to put the fear of God into you, but ADHD children who aren't medicated are the ones who usually cope at GCSE, invariably fail at A-level when they have to focus on fewer subjects, and if they manage to get through A-levels they nearly always crash at university because the stress and pressure of behaving in a way that your brain doesn't want to will always affect them in the end.

There's a lot of other reasons why ADHD kids struggle when it comes to university but for now, trust me, the ones on medication have a much better chance of making it.

There are tons of other very good reasons why it is sensible to at least try medication.

If your ADHD child is one who suffers with emotional dysregulation or anxiety, the medication, when it is working, can have a hugely positive effect. I would go so far as to say it can completely eradicate unstable moods and therefore lessen the likelihood of self-harm and suicidal thoughts. Unregulated ADHD teenage emotions can be extreme, and the medication can have a life-changing positive effect on emotionally unstable teenagers.

More positive benefits of medication are -

- They can motivate your child. Without even noticing it, your child will have a lot more motivation to do things, including the boring things!

- They should pretty much stop procrastination. Jobs and tasks that have been put off before will suddenly start getting done.

- Meds will allow your child to think a thought for long enough for it to be stored as a memory. So, things that up to now have regularly been forgotten, like lunchboxes and PE kits, should suddenly be remembered.

- They should also stop, or at least reduce, impulsivity. Your child is less likely to lose friends and they will upset fewer teachers by not saying and doing things impulsively.

- Your child should now be able to think of consequences. I can't begin to tell you how important this one is. If I tell you that most of the prisons are full of ADHD boys who didn't think of the consequence before committing silly crimes, you'll know that putting this ability back into your child's brain is critical and could very well be life-changing.

Have I convinced you that medication is a good idea yet? If not, I'll keep going! If your child has had any sort of binge eating problem, or uncontrolled eating, compulsively eating sweets, stealing or gorging on food - the medication will regulate their appetite.

Medication should also calm their brain and stop the racing thoughts. Most ADHD kids have brains that don't stop, and the medication will actually allow them to think one thought from the beginning to the end. This is a completely novel idea for anybody with ADHD who has constant crashing thoughts ricocheting round their brain. A calm brain has to be one of the best things the medication offers.

I can speak personally on this. On the few occasions I've tried ADHD stimulant medication the effect in my brain has been nothing less than earth-shattering. For the first time EVER, I knew what it felt like to have a brain that was calm, that wasn't incessantly thinking and overthinking. Quite honestly it was the best thing since sliced bread and although I have my own reasons at the moment for still struggling to be on stimulant medication, it is my absolute goal to get back on it because this affect is truly wonderful.

So now we can see the medication, when it works, is pretty fantastic but there have to be side-effects right? And yes, there are. I always say to people that ADHD medication has to be the hardest to get on BUT when you are on it and it is working it has to be the best in the world. I'm not exaggerating here because ADHD medication is known as the most efficacious of all medication - because it is the only one that replaces something missing in the brain.

But let's talk side-effects. There aren't that many, but they can be bad enough to turn people off the meds altogether.

I'll list these in the order they seem to affect the thousands of ADHD people I have now met and worked with -

▪ Sleep. There is quite a large portion of people who find they cannot sleep on stimulant medication. I've known people who have been awake for a week when they first take them. This is obviously very dangerous, and I send all of them straight back to their psychiatrist. Some psychiatrists will give you additional medication to counteract the effect of a stimulant. Melatonin is very popular with children and teens, and medication to calm your brain down at night can be very useful for adults. More than any other side-effects, I'm positive disrupted sleep has to be the top one.

- Lack of appetite. Now for some of us carrying a few extra pounds (who am I kidding, stones), this one isn't such a horror and it can't be a coincidence that the first line medication Elvanse for ADHD, is also prescribed for binge eating. Some people however find their appetite is wiped out to quite a dangerous degree. Kids can go days without eating and then only realise when they faint in school.

- Bad mood/meltdowns/anxiety when they wear off. Not so much with Elvanse, but other older-style ADHD medication can cause some people to have a terrible 'crash' late in the afternoon when it wears off. Parents report children suddenly becoming very angry, wired, emotional and this is the effect of the medication leaving their brain.

- Anxiety/chest pain/heart palpitations. This is rare but if it does happen consult your psychiatrist immediately. They will usually tell you to stop taking the medication and make an appointment to see them. It is rare but it does happen.

- Dry mouth and being constantly thirsty. It is recommended that you drink a lot of water when you are taking ADHD medication. For some reason it makes it work better. They also recommend that you have protein in the morning and at lunchtime if you are taking Elvanse. Apparently, that helps it work better too.

Something I come across a lot is boys in their late teens who have decided they no longer need their ADHD medication. I always meet the ones who have hit trouble as result. A lot of boys seem to think that they only needed the meds for school, and they are fine without them. Hardly ever is this the case. We now know that we are born with ADHD and we die with it. It is absolutely not a childhood disorder that you grow out of in your late teens. But this old urban myth still floats around and many with ADHD also believe it is true.

My therapy room is chock-a-block with 17-19 year-olds thinking they don't need the medication anymore and not yet linking their dismissal of meds to the fact their lives have gone very wrong.

Most parents have the devil's own job talking these headstrong teenagers back into taking medication. I have tried too and the best way I've found is to tell them they only need to try it short term. Try it for a week or two and see if it makes a difference. If it doesn't, they can just stop taking it. There is no long-term build up with ADHD medication so you literally can take it for a week or a fortnight and then stop with no negative impacts. Hopefully in this time they will have seen the difference being back on meds can make.

Medication isn't right for everybody, of course, but from what I've seen, it has a dramatically positive effect on most people with ADHD. Don't give up at the first hurdle. You might need to try two, or even more, different kinds of medication to find the right fit for your child, but generally speaking, the positive effects are numerous and worth persevering for.

DON'T EVEN THINK ABOUT . . . dismissing the thought of medicating completely.

WHAT WORKS BETTER . . . watch and monitor how your ADHD child is coping especially around temper, meltdowns, concentrating at school and emotionally. Keep an open mind about medication. Be prepared to try it and to change it as they mature. What works for them at 6 might not at 16.

What worked and what didn't?

WHEN YOU ARE WONDERING WHETHER AN ADHD COACH OR COUNSELLOR MIGHT HELP ... BUT DON'T HAVE A CLUE WHAT THE DIFFERENCE IS OR WHERE TO START

The good news is there is becoming quite a lot of choice when it comes to professional help you can access for your ADHD child. Be warned, most of this is going to cost you money. But there are some charitable organisations who offer therapeutic help for ADHD kids and their parents and in the 'help' section at the back of the book you will find details on some of those. But it can be a bit of a confusing quagmire of job titles and here I'm going to make sense of them for you.

ADHD COACH

This is somebody who is almost definitely not a qualified counsellor. If they were, they would mention it in the job title. An ADHD coach is likely to be somebody who has done a specific coaching course on everything ADHD. All of these at the moment are American and cost a small fortune. These coaches will be able to help you and your child understand all the ADHD traits they are dealing with and come up with the best tried and tested coping strategies and systems to overcome these issues.

What they won't be able to do is deal with emotions and feelings to the depth a counsellor could. They won't be trained in areas such as self-harm, suicidal ideation, self-esteem, body dysmorphia, eating disorders, anger management, anxiety, depression and a whole catalogue of issues. A counsellor will.

There are some very professional ADHD coaches available and they most certainly have their place. In my personal opinion, that place is working with adults who have no other issues aside from their ADHD traits.

ADHD COUNSELLOR / PSYCHOTHERAPIST

These people will have undertaken a minimum of three years and probably four/five years training in counselling/psychotherapy, often to degree and masters level. Somewhere along the line they will also have gained ADHD knowledge. This is nearly always because they are ADHD themselves and have chosen to specialise in this area. You will also find parents of ADHD children who are qualified counsellors, offering ADHD counselling services.

My advice here would be to always look at somebody's personal website. Don't go on one of the general ones and see that they have ticked ADHD as a client group they work with. In reality, this could mean they have worked with one or two ADHD children before and won't turn away clients with ADHD. It doesn't mean they specialise in it or even know much about it. Counsellors tend to tick all these boxes in the hope they will get more clients.

In my view, and very generally speaking, a child or adolescent is going to need a counsellor - not a coach. I think coaches are ideal when there are no emotional or additional issues but I've yet to meet a child with ADHD who isn't also suffering with low self-esteem, health anxiety, depression, eating issues, bullying, friendship group problems, self-harm or any one of another hundred issues.

I qualified as a coach before I trained as a counsellor. In our coaching training we were told that if a client presents with emotional issues we had to refer them to a counsellor. Now I am trained as a counsellor I can completely see why this is the case. There is absolutely no point in working with a child on just their ADHD traits if there are underlying issues and there nearly always are with ADHD. Let's think first of the 30% of ADHD people who have social anxiety. In counselling there are a lot of ways of working with anxiety, for example Cognitive Behavioural Therapy (CBT) is known to be extremely successful. An

ADHD coach will not have been trained in getting to the root of the client's anxiety, let alone know how to deal with it.

So, think very carefully whether your child just needs help purely with ADHD traits. If they do then an ADHD coach will be sufficient. But if there is anything else going on like anxiety, depression, problems with siblings, self-harm etc, it is much better they are seen by a counsellor who specialises in ADHD. And for that you ideally need a counsellor who is diagnosed ADHD themselves. Nobody will understand your child's brain like somebody with the same brain themselves. It is why my organisation will only employ counsellors who have an ADHD diagnosis to work with ADHD clients. What we hear from clients over and over again is that it is amazing sitting in front of somebody who understands their brain.

You will now find people who are qualified counsellors AND coaches. I am one of these. Until a few years ago that was pretty rare. Now it is becoming more common as the UK embraces coaching and counsellors are following up their training with coaching training. I did it the other way around and became a coach ten years before I became a counsellor. But you will find combined ADHD coaches and counsellors now, and personally I think that's your best option. The choices are out there for you to make.

CBT THERAPIST

This will be a professional who has undertaken specific Cognitive Behavioural Therapy (CBT) training. If they don't have ADHD themselves or a massive understanding of it, they aren't going to be much use to you.

ADHD PSYCHOLOGIST/PSYCHIATRIST

These people you will only usually sit in front of when you are looking for an assessment for ADHD or medication for the condition. Psychologists can diagnose the condition, but only psychiatrists can medicate. They don't usually offer any form of psychotherapy.

It is also worth mentioning at this point that your GP cannot prescribe ADHD medication. It has to come from a consultant at psychiatrist level. This is because (most) ADHD medications are controlled so that your regular GP can dispense prescriptions for them but cannot initiate a prescription for them.

What worked and what didn't?

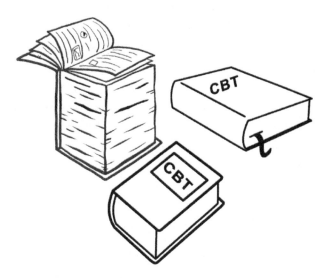

WHEN YOU KEEP BEING TOLD CBT IS THE ANSWER BUT HAVEN'T GOT THE FOGGIEST WHAT THAT IS

CBT stands for Cognitive Behavioural Therapy and you hear the term bandied about so much because the NHS in the UK has been using it as it is 'preferred choice' of therapy for a good few years. The reason they use it so much is because more than any other counselling method, CBT is evidence based - you go from A to B and you get a result. The NHS want to be able to evidence results.

So, what is it all about and can it help your ADHD sprogs?! My answer to that is a definite YES in almost all cases.

I'm going to go through the relevant elements of CBT here very much picking out the elements I think work brilliantly with ADHD kids. I've literally seen it work, and help, dozens and dozens of times. And it is simple enough for even a 10-year-old to grasp the basics.

If you want to go into CBT more thoroughly I can strongly recommend three excellent websites. These have tons of information leaflets, CBT exercises and even full CBT programmes that you can download. The programmes each specialise in one problem area. Examples are self-esteem, body dysmorphia, health anxiety, procrastination, worry and rumination, and there are loads of them. Each programme has around 10 to 12 modules and if your child has one real problem area, this is a free resource which will be almost definitely very powerful. See the useful info section at the back of this book.

However, if it is general CBT you'd like to get a handle on, keep reading! Broken down, CBT means 'cognitive' - your brain and how we think, 'behaviour' or how we behave and 'therapy' is changing for the better. So its basis is changing your thoughts to change your behaviour for the better.

You might have heard of the CBT hot cross bun. Before you reach for the butter and start salivating it is actually a Diagram - THOUGHTS, FEELINGS, BEHAVIOURS, PHYSICAL SYMPTOMS

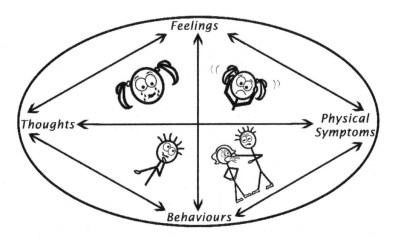

The theory is that whatever the problem, you can break the circle at any point to change the end result. Let's take an easy example. If your child is depressed their thoughts, when identified, might be 'I'm boring, nobody likes me I've got no friends'. This might leave them feeling sad, lonely and rejected which might lead to them isolating themselves, not going out, not answering the phone and staying in bed. Their physical sensations may be feeling sick and tired.

To break the cycle, a CBT therapist will enter the hot cross bun at the point where it can have the most effect AND where it is most do-able for the client. In this case I would suggest a behavioural change might have instant impact. Starting by answering the telephone and going out. Baby steps. This is the core CBT therapy. But the two areas I think are most helpful to your ADHD kiddywinks are as follows:

UNHELPFUL THINKING STYLES. This is massively relevant. One of the traits of ADHD is overthinking and ruminating. I've yet to meet one ADHD person who doesn't overthink to a lesser or greater degree. Many tell me it is the worst trait and the one that gives them the most grief. I believe it is responsible for nearly all the anxiety we suffer and can be life-threatening in its extreme. People who self-harm will always tell you it was their thoughts they were trying to escape from.

Some thoughts are positive. In CBT these are called Positive Automatic Thoughts (PATs). And the opposite to these are Negative Automatic Thoughts (NATs). These are the ones your child will need help recognising. And changing. And that's not as hard as you think. I recommend you have a look at the 12 most common unhelpful thinking styles. How many apply to you? If you start familiarising yourself with these, and start noticing and pulling yourself up on them, you'll be better placed to notice when your child does it and to help them to change their thought processes.

CATASTROPHISING. Always assuming the very worst. This is classic ADHD! Nothing is ever just a bit rubbish, it is always a total disaster! Instead, encourage your children to keep it real. What do they know? What are the possible outcomes not just the worst?

BLACK-AND-WHITE THINKING. Also known as All Or Nothing Thinking. Again, classic ADHD. For us everything is either brilliant or it is absolutely awful. Instead, try getting your child to look at grey areas. Are there any? How many different ways can you look at things?

MENTAL FILTER. Not seeing the full picture. Filtering out the good bits and only registering the bad. Instead get them to explore what they might have missed.

SHOULD AND MUST THINKING. Being hard on yourself by using phrases like "I should" "I must", "I ought to". Rarely is this thinking helpful. Instead try "it would be nice if", "I might" and "I could".

MIND READING AND FORTUNE TELLING. Thinking we know what someone is thinking or how something is going to pan out. Instead try staying in the now. Force your brain to think only of what you have evidence of.

EMOTIONAL REASONING. Assuming that because something makes you feel a certain way it must be true, for example "I feel stupid in maths so I must be thick". Instead try "I don't feel confident yet in maths so maybe I'd benefit from one-to-one sessions with a teacher or a private tutor".

OVER GENERALISING. Imagining something always happens based solely on one event. Typical ADHD. We can be dramatic! Instead, check out the evidence. How many times has it actually happened?

MAGNIFICATION AND MINIMISATION. Building other people up, putting them on pedestals. And belittling yourself or your own attributes/achievements/skills. This feeds in beautifully with ADHD's lack of self-esteem. Instead, remember you only see what other people want you to see. Very often people present very differently publicly. Instead, focus on yourself and know your own worth. There is no point second-guessing other people.

PERSONALISATION. Taking everything personally. Always thinking you are responsible, and everything is your fault. Instead, try looking around. Who else is involved, what part might other people have played in this?

LABELLING. Making global statements or assumptions about ourselves to others for example "everyone in my class is horrid because they all hate me". Instead, think who has ever been kind to me? Or helped me? Do they all deserve to be labelled?

And another thing. This statement I have found to be the most powerful one ever. Think about it for a minute . . .

A THOUGHT IS JUST A THOUGHT. IT IS NOT NECESSARILY A FACT.

This is crucially important to ADHD brains as we have more thoughts than most and a good portion of those are negative. But they are just thoughts. That does not mean they are true or factual. If you can get this bit of CBT into your child's head, you'll help them so much. An ADHD brain can fire off hundreds of thoughts in a day and if you can just get your child to understand that a thought really is just a thought it will do wonders for their mental health.

I'm a very big believer in CBT and there are hundreds of books on the subject. There are specifically books for using CBT on children so if you want to go further into this, I strongly recommend it. For me it is by far and away the best counselling method to work with ADHD brains.

What worked and what didn't?

BEFORE I LET YOU GO

Please don't feel abandoned! In the *Helpful Links, Books, Websites and Charities'* section at the end you'll find many people who really do understand ADHD and can help you. You might feel alone, but I promise you - you absolutely aren't.

Just take a very quick flick through the pages of this book. And remember: your ADHD child is dealing with ALL (or most) of this stuff 24/7. Life isn't easy when you are ADHD, but it can be made a whole lot easier by having a parent/parents who understand what is going on in your busy, fuzzy little ADHD head.

Remember you are one of the good guys! You are one of the parents who really wants to understand your child. I know that because you bought this book - Or maybe you nicked it off somebody but as long as you've read it - who cares!! The intent is the same.

My one overriding message to you will be to try and be on the same side as your child. Don't take up an opposing position. Make very sure they know you are on the same team. I've watched families crumble because the parents insist on taking an oppositional stance. It never, ever works. Whatever blend your family is, with however many parents, stepchildren, half brothers and sisters and whatever fusion you've got going on - YOU are family. And the ADHD child is one of YOU. They are not on the other team. So please don't ever give up trying to understand them. And always let them know that you are in this together.

More than anything I hope I've given you an insight into what is behind ADHD behaviour. Remember, no behaviour just appears. There is always a reason for it. And with ADHD there can be trillions of reasons, and combinations of several traits, which can make it very perplexing for parents and carers. But do not give up. Your ADHD child has the potential to be a Sir Richard Branson or a will.i.am, or any one of the millions of very successful ADHD people.

Thank you for being one of the committed people who has read this book - trying to do the best for your ADHD child. I applaud you. And I wish you the absolute best in bringing up your ADHD cherub to be a successful, confident, ADHD-aware thriving adult - who will almost definitely go on to have ADHD kids of their own. So, GO YOU! You've just learnt how to handle your grandchildren as well !!

HELPFUL BITS

BOOKS

- ### DELIVERED FROM DISTRACTION

  by Edward M Hallowell MD & John J Ratey MD, Ballantine
  Books 2005, ISBN: 9780345442314

  For adolescents/adults with ADHD or wanting to know
  more about adult ADHD. A brilliant book written by a
  psychiatrist with ADHD himself. Really easy to read even
  for those of us who can't concentrate to read books! Funny,
  incredibly informative, and highly recommended. I always
  say to the teens and adults I work with "if you buy only one
  book on ADHD, make it this one".

- ### THE ADHD EFFECT ON MARRIAGE

  by Melissa Orlov, Specialty Press/A.D.D. Warehouse 2010,
  ISBN: 9781886941977

  A fabulous book if your relationship is running into trouble
  because either one or both of you are ADHD. Doesn't just
  work for married couples. Also brilliant for people in new
  relationships when one or other is ADHD. Really helps you
  understand how the ADHD traits impact on relationships
  and best ways of rectifying things.

- ### TAKING CHARGE OF ADULT ADHD

  By Russell Barkley PhD, The Guildford Press 2010, ISBN:
  9781606233382

  This is a great book for teenagers and adults alike. Goes into
  lots of detail about ADHD and importantly gives you lots of
  different ways of overcoming individual traits. Really easy to
  read book and very useful tips.

- **SMART BUT STUCK**

by Thomas E Brown PhD, Jossey Bass 2014, ISBN: 9781118279281

This is an easy read book with some excellent strategies for children and adolescents who are getting stuck for whatever reason. Purely using case studies of teens he has worked with, it gives different ways of overcoming 'stuckness' from different ADHD traits such as lack of motivation, procrastination, perfectionism, inability to make a decision and more.

CBT USEFUL WEBSITES

- getselfhelp.co.uk

- psychologytools.com

- cci.health.wa.gov.au

AUTHOR'S WEBSITES

- www.HeadstuffADHDLiberty.co.uk

For when you are struggling with ADHD and Addiction or Crime. We have ADHD Psychiatrists, Psychotherapists, Substance Misuse Specialists, Counsellors, Family Mediators & a full team to help you overcome any addictions and to guide you through any legal difficulties you find yourself in.

- www.HeadstuffADHDTherapy.co.uk

All Diagnosed ADHD Qualified Counsellors, UK Wide, offering ADHD Counselling & Coaching to Kids, Adolescents & Adults. Before, during and after diagnosis.

GLOSSARY OF TERMS – WHAT DOES THAT MEAN?

- ADHD - Attention Deficit Hyperactivity Disorder. Currently diagnosed in three types in the UK
1. ADHD Primarily Hyperactive/Impulsive
2. ADHD Primarily Inattentive
3. ADHD Combined which is by far the largest category
- Anankastic traits - similar to OCD but without the negative thoughts attached
- ASD - Autistic Spectrum Disorder. Autism
- Aspergers - Now classified ASD. You'll see it used still but officially its now High Functioning ASD
- BPD - Borderline Personality Disorder. Now renamed EUPD Emotionally Unstable Personality Disorder
- BRAIN FOG - When your ADHD brain can't think clearly. Can be crippling for some, mildly frustrating for others
- CAMHS - Children and Adolescent Mental Health Services. NHS service for children and adolescents up to 18
- Comorbidity - A condition existing alongside ADHD. Most common are social anxiety, dyslexia, dyscalculia, dyspraxia, OCD and less common, bipolar and EUPD
- CD - Conduct Disorder
- DSPS - Delayed Sleep Phase Syndrome. Sufferers circadian rhythm is approximately four hours behind what would be classified as normal. So natural 'fall asleep time' is 4 am rather than 11-12 midnight
- EHCP - Education, Health and Care Plan
- EUPD - Emotionally Unstable Personality Disorder. The new name for Borderline Personality Disorder

- FAS - Fetal Alcohol Syndrome. Caused when a mother has used alcohol during pregnancy

- NT - Neurotypical. No neuro diversity present

- OCD - Obsessive Compulsive Disorder

- ODD - Oppositional Defiant Disorder

- PDA - Pathological Demand Avoidance

- Perfectionism - striving for flawlessness and setting high performance standards

- Psych - Psychiatrist, in this book with ADHD as a speciality

- RSD - Rejection Sensitive Dysphoria

- Social Anxiety - A common comorbidity especially for boys. Usually means being uncomfortable (or unable to be) in crowds, big venues or public transport

- SPD - Sensory Processing Disorder

Made in the USA
Columbia, SC
10 July 2022

63252660R00114